While each life situation is unique, there are some basic principles to guide your children. Find out what to do if . . .

Your child is lying . . .

Technique #14 "Lies Equal Double Trouble"
Uncover why he felt the need to hide the truth and set fair consequences that will discourage future lies.

A friend or a pet dies . . .

Technique #22 "If There's a Loss, Let Him be Sad"
Respect the natural feeling of sadness and manage it in a constructive manner.

She refuses to clean her room . . .

Technique #4 "Bagging the Nagging"
How to write a contract so that your children pick their own consequence if they break the deal.

. . . And more. Starting today, you can overcome even the most difficult standoffs with your child as you establish a more loving and understanding relationship.

25 OF THE BEST PARENTING TECHNIQUES EVER

MEG F. SCHNEIDER
JUDI CRAIG, Ph.D., Consulting Editor

St. Martin's Paperbacks

25 OF THE BEST PARENTING TECHNIQUES EVER

Copyright © 1997 by Meg Schneider.

Cover photograph by Peter Brandt.

ISBN: 0-312-96178-2

Printed in the United States of America

St. Martin's Paperbacks edition/May 1997

10 9 8 7 6 5 4 3 2 1

In loving memory of my mother, Sally.
I'll miss her techniques forever.

CONTENTS

Acknowledgment

I would like to thank Dr. Judi Craig for her humor, wisdom, generosity, and tremendous talent for talking about real kids in real situations with real parents. I did not want to paint ideal pictures. She helped me bring the truth to these pages and that is what I most wanted.

What Makes a Great Parenting Technique?

The short answer to this question is, one that works!

The long answer involves understanding what we mean, or *ought* to mean, when we determine that a parenting technique is effective.

Because it isn't just about getting your child to behave well, or do as you say, or reflect qualities you believe he should have. A good parenting technique is about more than that.

It's about communicating how you feel about your rights, your child's rights, and his desires and needs. It should convey your respect for him, a clear picture of your expectations, and your willingness to understand him. And it's also about building your child's self-esteem even as you are correcting him, admonishing him, disciplining him, or teaching him.

What happens during the technique as you are using it, even before you get results, is as important if not more important than the results.

Which is why this book is set up the way it is. It's not just about what to do. It's about understanding why you're doing it. How you are helping your child in a multitude of ways even as you strive for him to stop tantruming, try a new sport, taste a new food, cope with a disappointment, accept responsibility for his own actions, cease from lying, and more.

This book is about more than the technique. It's about how to bring up a child who feels good about himself and you. A child who can handle the many difficult challenges of life. And it's about how you as a parent, can protect the boundaries of each of you so that resentment is at a minimum, and the relationship between you is as positive as it can be.

HOW TO USE THIS BOOK

Underneath each TECHNIQUE there are four headings. THE TECHNIQUE, WHY IT WORKS, THE DEEPER MESSAGE, and SEEING IT IN ACTION.

THE TECHNIQUE section is simply what you do. What you might say. Suggestions about your demeanor. Pitfalls to avoid. For instance, how do you use humor to detoxify a situation? You want to keep it brief, warm, and watch for the signs that your child might be taking offense.

WHY IT WORKS explains the effect your technique is having, which renders it so potent. What unspoken message is your child receiving that makes him react well? How are you making it possible for him to put his best foot forward? How, for instance, is humor going to ease the situation? Why does a good laugh work?

THE DEEPER MESSAGE is the underpinnings of the technique. It's not about the technique itself but rather what it is reflecting about how you see your child and yourself, your expectations, and your beliefs on the subjects of morality, integrity, and life's vicissitudes. Humor, even in the most painful situation can be both appropriate and necessary. When you use it you illustrate your belief that even the most dire circumstances deserve a ray of light, if not simply to ease pain.

SEEING IT IN ACTION is the place in which the

technique and results are illustrated. It is regularly split into three age groups because, of course, what you do has to be adapted according to the developmental capacities of the child with whom you are dealing. A four-year-old may believe you are laughing *at* him quicker than the time it takes to say "HA HA," but your twelve-year-old, hearing a kindly worded jibe, might just laugh.

It's important to note in the SEEING IT IN ACTION sections that the dialogues and actions that represent the technique are abbreviated and only suggestions. Of course you should feel free to adapt all aspects of what you do to your own personality. The ideas brought forth here are meant to:

- Point out the significance of certain words or phrases you might choose.
- Illustrate the various ways the technique can be used to suit different situations and children.
- Make you aware of what to look for in your child as you proceed so that you can improvise on the technique to increase its usefulness.
- Help you recognize where the limitations lie. Children are not Pavlov's dogs and you are not a magician. Sometimes satisfying results are not immediately evident.

These techniques are not miracles.

But they definitely work.

And many techniques can be used interchangeably. There are a few that work for kids who won't try new things, and others for those who won't stop causing trouble. There are also a number that touch on a child's lack of responsibility, or respect for others. The very beginning of each technique suggests some issues it can address. But this is meant as a broad guideline.

You'll have to see what works best for you and your child. And that will depend a lot on who your child is. . . .

YOUR PARTICULAR CHILD AND THE UNIQUE TECHNIQUE

The children in this book are of varying temperaments. Obviously the emotional makeup of your particular child should be taken into consideration with everything you do or say. So should the particular "stage" he might be going through.

Techniques will always have to be adapted or perhaps not even used at all. The tone and body language you use for the READ MY LIPS technique may not be right for a very sensitive child. The simple piercing look could reduce her to tears. On the other hand, a very demanding child might take advantage of GO AHEAD! BEND A RULE. You would have to choose your "flexible moment" with great care (and not too much frequency!).

A child who is quick to feel guilt, may be unnecessarily hard on herself with CHOOSE YOUR OWN POISON and perhaps the only way to get through to an extremely forceful, headstrong child for whom TIME OUT IS A PRIVATE MATTER only works a tad, is the SHOCK VALUE technique. For a prideful child, who you suspect harbors a very vulnerable ego, LET THEM SAVE FACE is going to be critical.

And, too, your child's past history and the particular situation should play a part in the way in which you apply a technique. A rare small infraction that must be stopped needs to be handled differently from an habitual large one, even if the same basic technique is required. The first lie, in other words, does not require a double dose of consequence. A child who chronically lies needs a much stronger message.

But no matter what sort of child you have and what problem has appeared, one of the most important parts of laying down the boundaries of constructive and acceptable behavior, is being fair and reasonable.

THE BOTTOM LINE ABOUT CONSEQUENCES

No matter what, a consequence has to equal "the crime."

This is a critical part of parenting. Not to balance the two would create a myriad of problems:

- Your child could feel so resentful of the punishment that no time is spent on understanding and regretting his poor behavior.
- A consequence that is way out of line works against giving your child a solid sense of cause and effect.
- A too-stiff consequence will fail to confirm your child's sense of the relativity of all acts.
- Your child may become increasingly sneaky in an effort to avoid a consequence that he knows will be dreadful, rather than face up to his mistakes.

An appropriate consequence that has a clear beginning and end, allows your child to more clearly evaluate what he has done. It helps to put his actions in perspective. It also adds positively to his perspective on you.

You are, he will see, reasonable and realistic.

An unnecessarily harsh consequence would pit the two of you against each other. A fair one, would minimize the anger and maximize the element of understanding between the two of you.

And one other point about an unnecessarily harsh consequence. It can be quite difficult to enforce and as a result penalize you! It's not easy to insist your child will have no play dates for three weeks. You're going to be badgered a great deal. It's unrealistic to proclaim you're going to cancel the family ski weekend because of your son's behavior. In the end you won't do it, and you'll end up looking a little foolish.

There are three important points to keep in mind when naming a consequence, that will help things stay on an even keel:

1) If you are really feeling furious, don't name the consequence. Wait a while, until you've had a chance to cool off. Otherwise you might state a punishment that is neither fair, nor sensible. Of course you can always retract it, but it's much better not to get caught in that pattern. If you are terribly angry, simply say to your child, "There is going to be a consequence for what you've done. But I'm a little too angry now to come up with one that will be just and fair. I'll speak to you about this later, when I can think more clearly." Not only is this respectful of your child in that you are saying "You deserve, even when you behave poorly, to be treated

well,'' but you are modeling a constructive way to handle anger.

2) Design a *logical* consequence whenever possible. It doesn't make sense to pronounce there will be no desserts for a week if your son repeatedly refuses to clean up his room. However, declaring that he can only watch his favorite cartoon in the evening, *after* his room is clean, will work very nicely. A child who is habitually late coming home from school (lingering way past the half hour you allow him to just hang out), shouldn't be told he can't leave the house all weekend. It won't help him break the impulse to linger and socialize ad infinitum after school. However, telling him he has to return home directly after school for two solid weeks to prove he can be responsible, will. It's fair to insist he win back his half hour free ''hangout'' time. The point is you want a consequence not only to change a behavior. You want it to connect with the problem so that it has a more long-term impact on your child's thinking.

3) Remember that fear, humiliation, or abandonment should not be part of the consequence. Physical threats are unacceptable. Embarrassing or humiliating a child in front of other people or his friends is unacceptable. And threatening to cut her off from her friends or not talk to your child or an announcement that you are leaving, is inappropriate and frightening as well. A child does not need to be ''broken'' in order to learn a lesson. In fact, profoundly hurting a child might only leave him feeling worthless or

worrying that he is evil or wondering why you don't love him and what he can do to win you back. Or, especially in an older child, it could lead to very self-destructive behavior.

The bottom line? Make your consequence reasonable so your child has a sense of being treated fairly. Give it clear parameters so your child won't have a chance to badger you with, ''Can I turn on the TV yet?'' Be logical. When appropriate, create a consequence that doesn't punish as much as it works to correct a behavior. And if it is a serious infraction, stay calm, take the time to think through a consequence, and then make sure it's both enforceable and reasonably convenient for you!

Which brings up one other goal of *25 of the Best Parenting Techniques Ever.*

Part of parenting well is doing so in a way that makes your life easier. You can't parent well if you're not feeling in control, or if you're sacrificing too much, or if you're constantly angry, or if each of you are failing to appreciate the other's boundaries.

25 of the Best Parenting Techniques Ever is about more than just changing behavior. It's about bringing up a child with good values, a strong character, and healthy self-esteem. But ultimately, it's also about building a strong relationship between you and your child.

A good parenting technique is one that leaves you both feeling trustful and respectful of the other.

Used well, that is what each of these techniques will accomplish.

TECHNIQUE #1

FORGET ABOUT YOUR CHILD, CONTROL YOU!

WORKS FOR: ANYTIME YOU RESPOND TO A CHILD'S DIFFICULT BEHAVIOR WITH OVERCHARGED EMOTION.

THE TECHNIQUE

When, during a stressful interaction with your child, you can feel yourself about to explode both physically and emotionally, focus on you, not her. Recognize that the degree of your anger has to, at least in part, be due to other outside pressures, disappointments, and tensions and that it would be very unproductive, not to mention destructive, to visit the intensity of your cumulative anger on your child. But as you turn the attention to yourself, keep your child informed about what you are doing.

"I am going to my room now. I'm annoyed you haven't finished your homework but I also had a difficult day. I need a break. I'll deal with you on this in a little while when I feel calmer."

If you are dealing with a child younger than six, you will have to take a moment to "set him up" for your absence. Either flick on the television, settle him into a play activity, or see if another sibling can keep him occupied for a bit. Once he's settled, tell your child, "I'm tired and need to lie down for a moment. I don't want to yell at you.'' Then add, ''I'll be back soon!'' so that you don't trigger any abandonment fears.

Once alone, call a friend to vent, listen to some music, or take a hot bath. Do whatever it takes to allow yourself to physically and emotionally calm down. Then ask yourself important questions. What was it about Jimmy's look that got you so angry? Have I seen it on someone else before? Is it really so important that Judy finish her peas? If Peter hands in sloppy homework it's really his problem. Why do I have to worry about what the teacher thinks of me? Am I upset about something totally unrelated to Jimmy?

When you feel in control and have the sense that you have separated out your angry feelings into the compartments where they belong (your work, annoyance at a friend, a button that is getting pressed, or quite simply your child's lack of cooperation), then you can return to your child. Depending on the problem, in a calm fashion you can either talk through what is upsetting you about your child's behavior, find new solutions, or in the case of a young child, with your new, more relaxed attitude use humor (see technique #6) or for instance saving face (see technique #5) to resolve the conflict.

WHY IT WORKS

Exiting the scene to gain control of yourself keeps you and your child from doing a destructive jig. An explosion will only result in painful words, increased resentment, and a general breakdown in connectedness and communication.

Exiting also models emotional control. By first explaining and then doing something about your anger, you are illustrating self-awareness and taking responsibility for your actions. In short, you are showing your child how to handle difficult emotions with respect for everyone involved.

Your child, too, will have a chance to cool off. No longer using his energy to fend off your "attacks" he might brood at first, but shortly thereafter he, too, will see things through a more "evenhanded" prism.

He may actually approach you first in a conciliatory mode, having been chastened by your absence and surprised and somewhat educated by the way in which you departed. He, too, he may realize, needed some time alone.

And finally, your child will actually think more seriously about any infraction when confronted with your absence instead of your anger. He will understand that something has to "give" and not feel as backed into a corner. Both of you will have had time to "think."

THE DEEPER MESSAGE

It is frightening to see a parent out of control. Certainly a child may yell back, cry, or grow eerily quiet in response, but at her core, she will feel knocked off balance by your capacity to "lose it." In the last analysis if you are not her protector, who is? This is actually so for any intense emotion, such as deep grief or rampant anxiety, whether or not the emotion is directed at the child. Powerful emotions frighten children.

Explaining that you are feeling extremely tense is also

an important way of letting your child know that he is not responsible for everything. You are separate people and he should not have to cope with all of your negative feelings or experience guilt because of them. How you feel in many ways is your doing.

The same, of course, is true for him, a fact that will not be lost on him entirely, though he may understand this in a more primitive fashion. "I guess I should calm down, too," he might say to himself and with no small relief.

Watching someone out of control is an unpleasant experience. Feeling out of control is in many ways worse.

Finally, keep in mind two things. Your child is struggling with the desire to be close and yet separate from you. With some children this results in their desire to bait you. The fighting helps them stand apart. But the fighting might also be his way of covering up a deep insecurity or upset. If he fights with you neither of you has to focus on the real reason for his behavior.

In slowing things down, in standing apart, you are telling your child, "You can't pull this on me. I have a sense of what's really going on." And you will. The space will help you see the picture more clearly and your son see that he can't fool you. You will get to the truth or the essence of the problem.

He knows he needs you to understand him, and somewhere he will be grateful.

SEEING IT IN ACTION:

Your Four-Year-Old

Your son Will insists on picking out his clothes in the morning by himself. The problem is he has a way of yanking all the shirts out of the drawer until he finds the one he wants, and then leaving them there in a heap. You've repeatedly told him not to do so and lately he has seemed to be making an effort. Only a shirt or two lands on the floor and you've even seen him try to "fold" and return it to the drawer.

But this morning you walk in his room, after a poor sleep (caused by work problems) and you find his room looking like a bargain basement sale that's been picked over by everyone in town.

You turn to Will, who, oblivious, is struggling to snap the top of his jeans—a feat he has only recently, and proudly, mastered. But you don't care about that right now. All you can see is the mess, and your entire being is spinning out of control.

"I TOLD YOU NEVER TO DO THIS!" you announce, loudly stomping into Will's room.

Surprised and frightened by your tone, Will starts, and seconds later tears spring to his eyes. "YOU SCARED ME!" he cries out. "DON'T DO THAT!"

You force yourself to grow still. There's something out of sync here. Will is four, and you're looking at a messy floor, not a broken Ming vase. You are also interacting with a child who has no awareness of the consequences of his actions. The fact that you will have to take time out of your busy morning to put things away is simply not in his consciousness.

You take a deep breath. "I didn't mean to yell so loudly," you say. "It's just that I've told you that I don't want you pulling things out of your drawer, because then I have to put them back." You look at him not the floor. The floor is an infuriating sight. Much more so, you know, than it ought to be.

"I had to get my CLOTHES!" Will insists loudly, clearly not sure whether you're still in an angry mode.

"I'm going to go downstairs now," you say softly. "Finish getting dressed while I pour your cereal."

Then you go downstairs and instead brew a cup of coffee.

Ten minutes later you hear Will pad downstairs.

"Sorry, Mommy," he mumbles softly. "Can I have hot chocolate?"

"Yes." You smile at him. "But try very hard to remember not to pull all your clothes out? Because when you don't I have to spend SO MUCH TIME putting everything away and I need time to do other things, like go to the store and get your favorite dessert!"

He nods at you solemnly. "Oh," he says. "Okay. I like those sprinkle cookies . . ."

Your Nine-Year-Old

Alex has an extremely annoying habit. When he doesn't want to do something, he ignores you. He simply pretends he doesn't hear a thing.

You've been calling him from downstairs for the last five minutes to clean up the playroom. You know he can hear you. His door is open and twenty minutes ago when you passed by he was on his floor playing with Legos.

Finally, totally frustrated, you march upstairs and stand in his doorway.

"Alex," you say sharply. "Did you hear me?"

"No." He shakes his head, looking at you with a kind of guilty stubbornness.

"I said go down to the playroom and clean it up."

"OKAY . . ." he responds in an irritated voice. "But first I just have to finish this space invader ship with a . . ."

"I'm not interested in your ship." You can feel yourself spiraling out. You can actually feel yourself turning red.

And so you close your eyes for a brief moment and take a long deep breath.

"I am going to go down to the kitchen and make myself a cup of tea," you say quietly. "I feel as if I'm going to explode. When I am through with my tea I will expect the room to be clean, and if it is not, there will be no television for the rest of the weekend."

You turn and head downstairs, relieved.

Thoughtfully you brew the tea and heave a sigh of relief when two minutes later you hear Alex come down the stairs and head for the playroom.

After sipping the tea and reading a magazine article, you feel calm enough to find Alex, who is now sitting in the very neat playroom flipping through a toy catalog.

"Good job," you say matter-of-factly. "But, Alex, you have to understand that a dirty room is not half as annoying as being ignored. It's extremely disrespectful. If you don't start acknowledging me when I talk to you in the way that I acknowledge you when you talk to me,

I'm going to have to give you a consequence, which I never enjoy doing.''

"Yeah," Alex says without looking up. He doesn't like to give you much room.

"Look at me, please," you say quietly.

He does. Something in your calm is more powerful than your fury.

"Thank you," you say quietly and with a smile. "Would you like to play a game of Monopoly?"

"Yes." Alex nods enthusiastically.

"You listened!" You laugh brightly. A little humor (see technique #6) always helps.

Your Twelve-Year-Old

Lily doesn't seem to care about her schoolwork.

This afternoon she's brought home her third English paper with a grade of C. When you read it over you are quite sure she can do better. There are incomplete sentences, misspelled words, and the paper has little in the way of concluding thoughts.

You can't abide this. You were always a good English student and part of your advertising job now involves putting together copy. Good writing skills have always come easily and seemed monumentally important to you.

It infuriates you that Lily does not seem to care.

You are about to sharply reprimand her and then angrily sit down to go through the litany of what's wrong when instead you pause and remind yourself that so far this hasn't worked.

Yelling hasn't improved her papers at all.

And so you ask yourself a few questions. Does she have to be as strong as you in English? Is her teacher doing a good enough job? Does she even understand why writing skills are so important? Are the two of you now locked in a battle that prevents her from wanting to learn?

You put the paper down, sigh, and say, "This must not make you feel very good," and then open the kitchen cupboard to begin dinner. You need, you realize, to step away from the situation a little. "There has to be a way to improve things."

"I TRIED!" Lily insists, as if you've just yelled at her.

"You know, honey, maybe you did, but I want to think about how to help you and right now I've got to do something about dinner. I'll talk to you later when I have some constructive thoughts."

"I want to talk now," Lily persists. It's as if she wants a fight. A fight, you begin to suspect that will keep her from thinking about whether or not she could do better. After all, what if she tries and it doesn't work?

"I don't," you reply evenly as you continue with the meal.

You hear Lily angrily stomp from the room.

An hour later with the pasta boiling, the sauce under-way, and your business calls returned, you head upstairs.

"Lily," you begin, "I think we both need to approach this writing thing in a new way. I didn't want to talk to you then, because I figured I'd start shouting and that's pretty dumb. It occurred to me to have a conference with your teacher and see if I could get you a tutor for a brief period until you get your skills down." You place your hand on her shoulder. "Writing skills are very important. You'll need them at college and they count in almost any job. I don't want to fight about this anymore. I just want you to improve.''

''What if I can't?'' Lily responds almost accusatorially, as if you're trying to make a fool of her.

''Writing skills aren't magic. You can learn them. You don't have to be Ernest Hemingway.'' You say this confidently. You smile at your daughter.

She nods. ''I hate writing,'' she mutters.

You don't respond. This is the kind of invitation to dance you have to start turning down.

GIVE A LITTLE GOODNESS ITS DUE

THE TECHNIQUE

Most parents spend an inordinate amount of time focusing on their children's poor behavior. As a result they end up drawing attention to what they do not value, and fail to underline what they do.

Children often don't know as much as adults assume. Treating a sibling kindly, thanking someone graciously for a gift, or simply cleaning up a room does not immediately "read" to a child as commendable behavior. It takes some praise to underline the fact.

Too, simply focusing your attentions on poor behavior or even good behavior as a result of a threatened or actual consequence only leaves your child commanding center stage at moments of high drama.

He also needs that attention when he is simply being. This includes being told, "Wow, are you good company!" while the two of you are ambling through a park simply chatting together.

Praising good behavior that unfolds naturally during

the day, draws attention to spontaneous good. Words of praise reinforce these behaviors in a powerful way. "You two have been playing so well together today! I'm so impressed!"

While it's always good to start off with a reward that is more social than tangible, such as praise, on occasion you might want to include a small privilege or treat, to further reinforce the good behavior. "You were so polite at Grandma's today. I was so proud. You get to pick what we have for dinner tonight!"

When dealing with an older child, noting that a curfew has been met, or homework has been done will give you a chance to point out the positive connection between his responsible behavior and your willingness to give him more freedom. "You are really a very responsible person. It makes it easier for me to say yes to you when you want permission to do different things. I do like it when you have a good time . . ."

However, if it seems to you that there is very little during the day that inspires you to offer praise, and that, in fact, you are always finding fault it will be important for you to assess your expectations. It's possible that you are expecting too much and that you might have to begin praising behavior that is short of the mark, but on its way nonetheless. Your child may not clean his room at the end of the day quite the way you would like, but if he remembers to put his books on the shelves, his shoes in the closet, and his blocks in the can, that might be enough to merit praise. Too much faultfinding might also mean you are too involved. Some mistakes children are better left correcting on their own, encouraged by teachers and/or friends to do so. Too much parental intervention can build resentment.

It is important to remember that children are forever fighting an internal battle to be close with you and yet also, separate. Too much involvement will leave them needing to push away even harder and at moments when they might need you very much.

WHY IT WORKS

It is a fact that children will go for negative attention instead of no attention. Praise cuts them off at the pass.

It is also a fact that everyone operates more constructively when they receive compliments. It's inspiring. It builds self-confidence. And quite simply, it feels good.

If you find yourself constantly criticizing your child, unable to see when he is, in fact, being perfectly lovely, this technique will also help you slow down and consider things from a less demanding perspective. If you look for the good, you will undoubtedly find it. As a result of your praise not only will your child continue to do what you clearly value, but she will very likely begin to work toward more positive behaviors in other ways as well.

Your older child, clearly seeing the relationship between his mature behavior and privileges, will sense your respect and trust and rise, with limited conflict, to the occasion.

It is very easy for children to feel as if they can't do anything right. Praise will give them a sense of their own strengths.

THE DEEPER MESSAGE

Children need to see that you approve of them. It is a necessary component to the development of positive self esteem.

When you praise children for a behavior, or a quality in their personality, not only do they learn more clearly what it is you value, but they themselves feel appreciated. It is a wonderful feeling to spontaneously behave in a particular way and find that without even trying you have done something "good." It is a reinforcement of your child's basic sense of self.

And, by focusing on the good instead of just the bad you are telling your child, "I see all of you." When your child senses that you are aware of and happy about his goodness he will not feel as inclined to grab your attention in a negative fashion. He will feel comfortable with what you see in him because it's a vision the two of you can feel good about.

Keep in mind your child doesn't and shouldn't need to feel perfect, or for you to see him that way. Your constant negativity, however, can leave him feeling that perfection is what you want and that he is woefully inadequate. When you note the good and bad the underlying message is that he can be many things at once. One does not negate the other.

This is a profile he can live up to.

SEEING IT IN ACTION:

Your Four-Year-Old

Ezra's teachers report he cleans up nicely at school. This makes it extremely difficult for you to understand, why at the end of the day, you cannot get your son to straighten up his room.

The scenario is always the same. After his bath you tell him it's time to clean up. He says okay, then walks into his room and starts to play. It looks belligerent to you, and so you usually raise your voice. Pretty soon he's crying while you're cleaning up, repeatedly informing him, "I'm very angry that you don't clean up this room." By the time you've finished he's managed to toss a few super figures into a large blue toy chest. But that's it.

It now occurs to you that something about this room cleanup might be too daunting.

Tonight, after his bath, you walk into his room and look around. It's utter chaos. "You know," you begin with a thoughtful tone in your voice, "this is a lot to clean up. Let's each take an assignment."

"What?" Ezra asks, clearly mystified. Something different is going on, but he's not sure what.

"I'll put away the cars and trucks," you say, "and you collect your figures and put them in their box. How about that?"

Ezra, having been given a manageable task begins picking up his figures.

"Thank you, Ezra." You nod your approval as you

slip the books onto the shelf. "Good job!"

Once each of you have completed those tasks, you move on to another two. Again you praise him. "That's right. Your dirty clothes go in the hamper. Excellent!"

In about five minutes the room is nicely neatened up. The two of you survey the room.

"There you go!" you say happily. "You took good care of your things."

Ezra nods proudly.

He feels good, you realize, because you'd loosened your expectations and given him goals he could easily reach. At school he has lots of helpers. Everyone has a particular job. Simply telling him to clean up his room, was too complicated and lonely a task. It had made him feel unsure and inadequate. By slicing up the pie, you put him back in control and gave him a chance to feel able and very appreciated.

Your Eight-Year-Old

Ali usually spends a lot of time bickering with her younger sister. If they aren't fighting about their toys, they're accusing each other of name-calling or pushing.

It seems like every time they are together for more than half an hour, you end up yelling a lot and distributing time-outs like soda at a baseball game. By the end of the afternoon, everyone feels miserable, persecuted, and unloved.

Sunday afternoon arrives and Ali's play date cancels. Unhappily she trudges upstairs and seconds later you hear her and her sister chattering away. This, you assume, will last for about fifteen minutes. You pick up your favorite magazine and by the time you're through with all the articles you realize an hour has gone by.

And yet you don't hear a sound.

Quietly, you tiptoe upstairs and find your children hunched over a huge box of Legos, building a castle. You stand and watch this scene for a moment and then say softly, "That's beautiful!"

"It is," Ali says. "We're not through yet."

"You're working together so well," you go on. "That's so great to be able to do things like a team. The castle will end up being so wonderful . . ."

"We know," Mia intones, puffing out her chest just a little bit.

"I'm glad you know," you answer and then turn and walk down the stairs.

The afternoon is quiet for another hour. And then suddenly the bickering begins. You walk upstairs to find them arguing over crayons.

"Well, you two had a great afternoon. I'm so proud of you. But you know what? I think it's probably time for each of you to do something on your own. Let's divide up the colors so you can draw separately."

At first they agree, but then Ali, standing up petulantly insists, "I want to draw with Mia."

"Me too," Mia chimes in.

"Well, if you think you can do it as cooperatively as you built the castle, great! I know you can," you say encouragingly. "You just have to do it."

And then you leave the room.

Fifteen minutes later you still haven't heard a peep.

A little praise, you realize, and they're going for broke.

Your Twelve-Year-Old

Left to his own devices, Josh would consistently hand in messy homework. But you rarely leave them to him. You simply cannot bear to let him walk into school with work that reflects so little interest, pride, and sense of responsibility.

So almost every evening you hover nearby making sure he redoes his work, all the while saying, "I can't believe you're not embarrassed to hand in such sloppy stuff!"

But this evening you decide to step back and survey his homework in a different way. This pattern has to stop. He can't be all bad.

You don't jump at the messily scrawled essay nor do you shake your head at the large gray cloud of eraser marks on his math. You glance at the beginnings of a map he is drawing of Australia for a project. The shape, freehand, is quite good, the mountain range is cleanly penciled and though you suspect he hasn't gotten as far with it as he should have tonight, it's so far, neatly wrought.

"Wow," you breathe admiringly, overlooking everything else for the time being, "This is very good. It isn't easy getting proportions right. Good for you . . ."

Josh shrugs. He's not used to praise and is waiting for the other shoe to fall.

"If I were you I'd feel very proud of this map. I'm certainly proud of you." You don't even glance at the messy math paper you have noticed out of the corner of your eye.

And then, patting him on the shoulder in a congratulatory way you leave his room, not requiring him to redo his other assignments. You note the next morning that he is packing up the messy pages to take to school.

But you keep your own counsel. You've allowed him to see that when he gets his act together you are going to notice, and that you are quite sure he can.

He has your vote of confidence. The rest is up to him. Besides, hopefully the teacher will put on some pressure. It's okay to let her be the "heavy" sometimes!

GO AHEAD, BEND A RULE!

*WORKS FOR: UNUSUAL REQUESTS—SPECIAL OCCASIONS—
SURPRISE INVITATIONS—MORAL CRISIS—AND OTHER
MOMENTS, THAT CHALLENGE WHAT SEEMS TO BE
ETCHED IN STONE.*

THE TECHNIQUE

Recognize life's unpredictability by bending a rule. But at the same time, make it clear the moment is an exception. Always explain why and if necessary accompany the bent rule with a stipulation. "Okay, you can go out on a school night with your friend and his family for dinner this one time because I know Japanese food is your favorite and you have almost all your homework done. But the moment you get home you have to finish up."

Expect with your younger child that when tomorrow comes he or she may demand the same extra cookie or TV show. Just be very matter of fact. "Yesterday I rewarded you for doing such a good job helping Mom clean out your closet. But the rule is one cookie." If he throws a tantrum, simply say, "If this is the way you are going to act when I bend a rule, I won't be able to bend them anymore, so please stop."

Even your older child might press his luck and ask

for another exception right away. But if he does, try and listen to the particulars of the situation, putting aside your fears that anarchy is about to descend. Sometimes two bent rules in a row are necessary! But if it isn't, say so, and explain why. "I let you hang out with your friends longer than usual last week because you were celebrating the basketball win. There's no particular reason for it today and you need to get your homework done."

Finally, it is important to consider a moral dilemma. This is a situation where there is a principle you feel quite strongly about, but in order to help your child, it has to be if not quite put aside, then modified. Do it, but with a coda. Perhaps your six-year-old is terrified of visiting his sick great-grandmother. You ask him to do this only once a month, and you feel it's important, but he's going through a difficult stage now and something tells you not to push, even though family values are critical to you. You may elect to let him sit this month out, as long as he draws a picture for his great-grandmother you can take to her. You will be saying, "I think you should go, but I can see you're upset and that's more important to me. However, you will have to do something that is not so upsetting to you and which will make great-grandma feel good."

WHY IT WORKS

When a parent fears losing control and rigidly sticks to rules no matter what the circumstances, he boxes his child in. He makes the child feel as if he has no say in anything, and that the specifics of his life matter little next to a parent's edict. Continual rigidity only results in intense anger, resentment, and even depression. There is a certain lack of respect for your child when there is no flexibility. And there is confusion as well. A parent who fails to acknowledge the realities of life can be very distressing. Your child will feel lost, having to live by an unchanging set of rules in an unpredictable world.

A lack of rigidity, however, is an expression of trust in, and understanding of, your child. It is a sign that you are listening and watching and caring. There is no rule that is more important than him. You are also saying that parents don't always have to "win." There are times when your child's needs or desires can "overrule" a rule.

As a result of your flexibility your child will feel a sense of power. He was able to communicate his special needs and you heard them. This means he can speak out for himself and sometimes triumph. And when he doesn't, and this is key, he is likely not to feel beaten down or disregarded. His reactions to your "no" may not be happy or totally accepting ones, but there will be a backdrop of goodwill to his disgruntled response that will help him move on. He will remember that you do know there are times to bend and realize that sometimes the two of you will see these moments eye to eye and other times you won't. Naturally, he will keep trying to move you, and that's okay! Children almost always enjoy pushing the envelope but the truth is if they managed every time they wouldn't be happy with the chaos.

So have no fear of losing parental control. Your kids don't want you to anyhow.

THE DEEPER MESSAGE

The world is not just black and white. There are many shades of gray. This is a critical message to convey to your children. Your flexibility will lay the groundwork for your child developing realistic expectations of life. She will realize that things happen, both good and bad, and people have to find ways to accommodate them. Your flexibility will also help her relate better to others and to form deep and meaningful relationships. It is important in any friendship to put your needs occasionally aside, to be reasonable in one's demands, and to be forgiving of others.

Your flexibility will also help with your children's own decision-making skills when you are not around. The message is that sometimes, one has to go against what has always been. Children who are not exposed to this thinking may find themselves unable to budge from a position or have any faith in their sense of an unusual moment and its demands. A grief-stricken friend, for instance, asking a child from a rigid home, for some comfort might find himself put off because the child thinks he should go home to finish his work . . . torn though he might feel. But a child who has experienced flexibility will feel easier about making the judgment call that the friend at this moment is more important. (Hopefully you've told your child if he's ever going to be late, to call!)

This is not to say that your child may not occasionally deem something an exception, which, in fact, is not. But it is far better that he learn to consider every situation with an independent mind than to follow a rule blindly and with no regard for others. As for the moral dilemma, so much depends on the particulars of the situation. A child who chronically hands in work late because she gets distracted will not be aided by your willingness to help each time. But, generally speaking, if you have always had a "hands-off" policy about your daughter's schoolwork and for the first time she suddenly finds herself up against the clock, it is an opportunity to express her paramount importance to you. A principle, which she knows you hold dear, can be bent, out of love and your willingness to see her as a good person who has made a mistake and needs your help. There is a trust that can evolve from this sort of moment that will last forever, because you will have said, "I put you first."

SEEING IT IN ACTION:

Your Four-Year-Old

You have a rule at night. Only one cookie after dinner. Otherwise, you've noticed your four-year-old is catapulting off the walls for the rest of the evening and has a difficult time settling down to sleep. This particular evening, however, he has a friend over. They feel as if they're having a party, and both come galloping over to you filled with high spirits exclaiming, "Can we have two cookies! Please!!"

"Well," you remind your son, "you know I usually only allow one cookie."

"Oh PLEASE, PLEASE!" he exclaims. "I'll be

good! I won't get hyper!'' (You often tell him the reason he can't have it is that it makes him hyper.)

"Well," you say, smiling at him and the other child, "This does seem like a special night. You two never have dinner play dates, right?!"

"Yeah, never!" they both agree.

"Okay, then," you say, "a special night deserves a special treat. Two cookies for each of you." Give them the cookies and then before they run away, tap your son on the shoulder lightly and with a smile say, "Remember, we go back to one cookie after dinner tomorrow night. Right?"

"Right," he says.

And he may indeed expect just that. But if the next night, your four-year-old insists tearfully that he needs two, just calmly remind him of what was special about the night before, and that you had told him the one cookie rule still holds.

"No, you didn't," he insists.

"I know I did," you reply, and then add, "Please get a hold of yourself because next time there's a special reason for a special treat, I'm not going to want to break the rules. . . ."

This should help. You will have let him know that there will be other times when things will go his way, but that his part is to accept the times when they don't.

Your-Nine-Year-Old

You have an agreement with your daughter that since she is now in third grade, she will come home, have a snack, do her homework, and then she can go out and play. This has been going along reasonably well lately because the October days have been rather cold and dreary. But suddenly today the weather has turned balmy and other kids are out on the street biking. Your daughter no sooner walks in the house when she cries out, "Please, can I go biking, too!"

"What about your homework?" you ask. You're curious to see if she's got a plan in mind regarding her responsibilities.

"Uh . . . well . . ." she begins, clearly without a plan, "I could do it after dinner!"

"You have too much homework to do it all after dinner," you respond, "and you'll be too tired to do a good job. However . . . how about this? You can go biking now for an hour, and then I want you inside to do some of your homework before dinnertime. I realize it's a beautiful afternoon and you don't want to miss this chance to be outside. I don't blame you. Do we have a deal?"

Your daughter says yes and flies off to the garage.

An hour goes by and she, of course, does not come in of her own volition. You step outside, wave her over, and say, "Okay, an hour's up. Time to get started on your work."

"Oh please!" she begs you. "Please! This is so much fun!"

"I know you're having fun," you reply, "and I'm glad of that. But you have responsibilities at school and you have to fulfill them. Now bring your bike inside."

"I don't want to . . ." she whimpers. "You're mean."

"I'm not mean," you answer. "I'm pretty nice actually. And if you don't meet your deal with me, the next time there's a good reason to make an exception for you, I won't do it."

This should end the argument pretty fast, and again, on a positive note with just a touch of threat. Basically you have said, "I'd like to be flexible again. I'd like you to have your way occasionally. But not if every time I do, you make me sorry I did."

Your Twelve-Year-Old

You have a rule about the telephone. Neither your twelve-nor fifteen-year-old are allowed on the phone for more than forty-five minutes each night. They have their own phone and you think this is a very flexible arrangement. But now your fifteen-year-old has come home from school with a broken heart and clearly needs comfort from her friends. Tearfully she trudges up stairs calling down, "Mom, I really need to talk to Janie and Lisa, okay?" You know this means she'll be on way over the limit, but it seems to you that this is an evening to make an exception.

Your twelve-year-old, however, does not see it this way. Overhearing the conversation she calls out, "Only forty-five minutes!"

Her sister doesn't reply, having sunk into a grief-stricken world of her own. But you have to.

"I think we're going to bend the rules tonight," you say. "Your sister is upset."

"Okay, well then I get to talk more, too," your younger daughter insists. "Fair is fair."

"Nope," you answer. "The situations are not the same. Besides," you add with a little humor, "from the looks of your sister you won't get a chance to go near the phone anyway."

''Not funny,'' your daughter insists. ''I'll just call more tomorrow.''

Patiently you sit down, look your daughter squarely in the eyes, and say, ''Look. I am making an exception because your sister has special needs tonight. You don't. If you did, I would do the same for you. You can count on that. This rule of forty-five minutes is still in place. It's just that sometimes unpredictable things happen in life and feelings sometimes take priority over rules. In fact, your sister may have to talk a little more tomorrow night, too.''

Chances are your daughter will walk away from this conversation grumbling, but understanding things nonetheless. She will also have had it underlined for her that she can count on you to be firm, but feeling. That's a wonderful thing to know about one's parent.

As for your teenager, it's not necessary to march upstairs and remind her that she's being let off the hook because she has a broken heart, and not to expect this every evening once the crisis is over. True flexibility in this case is not reminding her of the reasons for your kindness, or warning her when it's going to stop.

Rather, it's knowing that sometimes things don't have to be said.

TECHNIQUE #4

BAGGING THE NAGGING OR
HOW TO WRITE A CONTRACT

*WORKS FOR: GETTING DRESSED—TAKING BATHS—DOING
HOMEWORK—COMPLETING HOUSEHOLD CHORES—PHONE
USE—EATING MEALS—CLEANING UP—PRACTICING A MUSICAL
INSTRUMENT—AND MORE. . . .*

THE TECHNIQUE

Don't nag. If you have to repeat yourself, change your
tone from a NAG to a REMINDER. A nag sounds annoyed and challenging. A reminder sounds helpful. You
are on your child's side.

Be sure to offer a zone of free choice. "Remember to
clean your room before dinner," gives your child
breathing space. As often as possible try not to demand
something on the spot. No one responds positively to a
dive bomber.

Use consequences carefully. For the younger child,
wait until the time is almost up and nothing has been
done, and then calmly, lay out a consequence. But lead
with the positive. "You can watch TV when your bath
is finished," is fine. "No TV until you've had a bath,"
is not. A consequence immediately offered to a young
child who has barely exhibited a reluctance to do something, is like saying, "Here's what I'd like you to do,

but I think you won't, so here's what'll happen when you don't.''

However, if you have been engaged in an ongoing battle, which you now want to stop, a consequence set out early on can only help.

When talking to an older child (a preteen), negotiate a contract complete with consequence (assuming this is a battle you've been waging for a while), making the rules clear. Then smile . . . and walk away. Your older child will only hear a reminder as a nag.

Then, and this is critical; should the time come and go and the ''job'' is not done, simply follow through with the consequence. No discussion. A contract is a contract.

Finally, for any aged child, offer an explanation as to why something has to get done. ''The lawn needs to be watered in the morning. Otherwise the sun will scorch the grass.'' Or, ''You have to take your bath by eight because you need time to pick a book, get into bed, and read a little while.'' Kids think parents just want to bug them. If you can explain yourself a bit you may lower the tension between you.

WHY IT WORKS

Nagging is not just the constant repetition of a request. Even when teamed with a ''please,'' it has a demanding quality.

An ever-honking horn, that anyone would want to shut out.

The problem is, no one likes to be controlled and no one likes being told what to do, especially if the ''assignment'' isn't fun. The more you push, the more likely your child, of any age, will want to resist.

But not just because he or she doesn't want to do it! Constant nagging turns up the temperature of any situation. A challenge is created. Who's going to give? Who's going to win? ''What will she do exactly if I don't shampoo my hair? If my math homework isn't done? If I don't get off the phone?''

Before you know it you're at the consequence-giving stage, which by its very nature makes you adversaries with your child. Not to mention points out who's boss. Of course there's nothing wrong with making that clear on occasion. But as noted earlier it's better to cast yourself as wiser, and able, and in control, than ''master of all you survey.''

It's also important to be mindful that children are forever experiencing an internal battle to be close with you and yet not too dependent. Nagging creates an opportunity to pull away. But it's a negative opening. As much as possible you will want to help your child reach for his or her independence in a less conflict-ridden atmosphere. Giving your child some breathing room, the sense of some choice, will help considerably.

By setting a limit that allows for some leeway, by reaching a joint agreement, and by sticking to your part of the bargain, you will be refusing to do battle. You will not have behaved as if your expectation is that your child will refuse to do as you have asked.

You will have removed the challenge.

You will have said, ''Here's what I need you to do. There's room. Let's work it out.''

While it may take a few consequence-receiving moments to get your point across, you will find that your child gets whatever it is, done.

As for explaining why you want a job done, sometimes when you tell a child something has to be done they only experience the demand. They don't consider its logic, wisdom, or practicality. If you can keep a purpose in front of your children they will be more likely to temper their resentment with an awareness of why something has to be done.

"Do it because I say so," only establishes your wish for authority.

But you can't just grab that. A child has to give it to you.

Nagging and demanding may get you what you want for the moment. But what you want most of all is a way to operate with your child that does not necessitate a battle of wills. What you want is mutual respect.

THE DEEPER MESSAGE

By setting forth your request in a reasonable fashion, recognizing your child's right to exercise some control, you are telling her that you know she can be responsible. That you expect she can make a positive choice. Nagging suggests a child doesn't have the sense to remember. It discounts a person's willingness to cooperate.

And so in a way you, as a parent, get what you deserve.

A gentle reminder to a younger child is a way of saying, "I want to help you get things done. I know you get busy with other things, but keep this task in mind." It builds a kind of camaraderie. You're not just telling her what to do. You're assisting her in getting it done by helping her disengage from one activity to take on another.

The consequence, if it comes to pass, will not feel so much as a punishment then, but as the unpleasant end to a chain reaction. And one he has to take responsibility for. Even if he argues, even if she screeches and runs to her room, both children will know the truth.

They had a part in the fiasco. They made the wrong choice.

In short order they will likely begin to make the right one.

SEEING IT IN ACTION:

Your Four-Year-Old

Your four-year-old has to get dressed for the day, but he refuses, with his newfound sense of "I can do," to allow you to pick his clothes or help him into them. You need to leave the house in forty-five minutes and he is busy playing with his action figures, which are now strewn all over his room.

"Honey," you can begin, "I need you to get dressed. We have to leave in a very little while." (Don't go into forty-five minutes. His sense of time is simply not there.) "Do you want me to help you?"

"No! I can do it," he answers. "First this guy has to get that guy."

"Fine," you say, surveying his room. "Finish up your game and then get dressed. But do it very soon."

You leave his room.

About five minutes later it appears he hasn't budged, and so you go back to him. "I think that Skullface must have gotten Brainman by now. You really do have to get dressed."

"I know, I know," he says. "But they're not dead yet."

"Well then why don't you have them decide to finish off their battle later? Try that, and then pick out your clothes. Otherwise, I'm going to have to take them from you."

You leave once more, give it about ten minutes and when he still hasn't made a move you go into his room and calmly sit down.

"I need you to get dressed now, because we're going to go shopping for Grandma's present. I am happy to let you pick out your own clothes and to get dressed yourself, but you don't seem to be doing that. You keep playing with your figures. Put them down now, get dressed, and then if you do that quickly enough, there may still be time for you to play."

"But I want to play!" he wails at this point.

And so comes the consequence. "Well, then I'm going to have to take away your figures, pick out what you're going to wear myself, and get you dressed." At this point bend down and pick one up to illustrate your point. "I don't want to, because I know you won't like that. But you've played and now we have other things to do."

"Okay," he mutters. Reluctantly he stands up and moves toward his dresser drawers.

Your Eight-Year-Old

You would like your eight-year-old to finish his home-work by six-thirty. After that you feel it will be too hard for him to go to sleep as his mind needs time to unwind. So you give him an option:

"Charlie, I want you to get your homework done be-fore seven o'clock. After that it's too hard to concen-trate. You get home from school at three, and we eat at five-thirty. I know you like to play a little, too. So, how do you want to manage this? You can do all of it after a snack and then play if there's still time, or you can do some of it after a snack, play, and finish up whatever's left right after dinner."

"I'll do some now," he says, "and then finish after dinner."

"Okay," you reply. "But remember you don't have that much time after dinner, so get as much as you can done now."

"Okay," he responds, while gulping down some cookies. Then he scurries upstairs.

Perhaps a half hour later he's down again, and drib-bling a ball outside.

Again, in a helpful tone you call out, "Finished most of your homework? After dinner doesn't leave you much time!"

"Right," he responds. "I know."

And so dinner comes and goes and you now notice that Charlie is dawdling, teasing his younger sister, and flipping through a comic book.

"Your homework, Charlie?" you say smiling. "Re-member?" It's time to throw in a motivating consequence. "If it isn't done by seven, no TV tonight."

"Yeah, I'll do it," Charlie replies.

Time passes.

You check the clock. It's six-forty.

And so the consequence.

"Okay, well, you made your decision about how you wanted to do your work. And I told you my one rule. You need to have it done by seven. No TV tonight."

He may run right up and try to beat the clock, or he may not.

If he doesn't and seven rolls around, ask to see what's not done. Insist he go upstairs and finish it, stick to no TV when it's done, and if he can't indeed finish it, set his alarm for a half hour earlier so that he can complete his homework first thing in the morning.

He had a hand in the plan, and fair warning.

And you were as evenhanded about it as you could be.

Your Twelve-Year-Old

Your twelve-year-old knows that every other day it's his turn to do the dishes. The trouble is he hates it and so every other day you end up nagging him endlessly. Only after the two of you are no longer speaking does he angrily march into the kitchen and do the "dirty deed."

Your twelve-year-old is fully capable of making a contract with you, and especially primed to argue with you. Which is why the contract part is so important. It's a kind of objective party. But there's something else. He's old enough to understand that you don't enjoy nagging. That it is as unpleasant for you as it is for him, and that you want this kind of interaction to stop.

Sit down with him and explain everyone in the house is busy with responsibilities and household chores that have to be shared. You understand he has a lot of things on his agenda and so you're willing to be flexible. He doesn't have to pop up directly after dinner and clean up, but on the other hand you don't want dirty dishes sitting around all evening, attracting bugs and sending off odors. What does he suggest? If he could tell you when he's going to do them you won't need to bug him. And use the word "contract." It carries weight.

"I can't bear bugging you anymore. Let's have a contract. We can do it verbally. We'll start with when you will commit to doing the dishes."

"I'll do them right before I go to bed," he says after rolling his eyes at your legalese.

You remind him this won't do. "That's on the late side and I don't want the dishes sitting for that long. They start to smell."

"Okay, then after my favorite TV show," he bargains.

If this is acceptable to you (try not to force your ideal moment upon him) then repeat what you've agreed to. "Okay, that means every other night, after you've watched *Video City* you will come into the kitchen and do the dishes. I will not have to ask you to do it. Do I have that right?" (Be sure to include clearly in the contract that this has as much to do with you not having to bug him as it does with the job.)

If he nods, given both of your awareness of his loathing of the chore, it's fair to suggest that you include in this contract a consequence.

Humorously say, "Okay, now since we both know how much you adore doing the dishes, and since we now have an agreement, what do we do if you don't get the dishes done? If I have to ask you to do them?"

He shrugs at that, but you give him a little push.

"It's important that you have a hand in the consequences as well as the dishes. I mean it. What do you think should happen if you don't get them done after the show and I have to remind you?"

He may or may not come up with something, but in any case you should select a consequence together and make it connected to the issue. Perhaps he will have to do the dishes two nights in a row, or, he will have to miss his favorite show the following night even though it's not his dish night.

Keep it reasonable, but stay firm.

The point is nagging is no fun for anyone. A young child won't understand how you feel about it. He needs positive assistance in getting things done. A middle-age child has some sense that nagging annoys you, but his self-discipline is still very erratic. It's fair to expect a few reminders will be necessary, but after that, it's also fair for him to accept a penalty. The preteen is entering a serious time of rebellion and is developing a heightened sense of what makes people tick. Let her know this nagging thing is over. Give her some space to sort out how to resolve the problem, let her know you think her capable of honoring a commitment but at the same time gently hint you know she'll be tempted not to, by constructing a "contract."

And whatever you do stick to that consequence. Otherwise you will be honoring your child's ability to do exactly as she pleases.

TECHNIQUE #5

LET THEM SAVE FACE

WORKS FOR: HEATED ARGUMENTS—WHEN MISTAKES ARE MADE—WHEN IT TURNS OUT YOU'RE RIGHT—WHEN YOU WANT YOUR CHILD TO STOP DOING SOMETHING—WHEN YOUR CHILD IS EMBARRASSED—AND MORE . . .

THE TECHNIQUE

While the situations above might hardly seem related, one thing is true about your child's needs in each. He will be far more apt to back down, admit a problem, or simply switch gears, if you let him keep a little power. If you want him to stop bouncing the ball and you've said so twice and now it's time to really stop, let him defiantly give it one more smack before he puts it away. If you're arguing a point and he looks it up in the dictionary and you're right, let him know you could see why he thought it was the other way around.

Don't present yourself as all-knowing, but rather as someone who happens to have known a particular thing at a particular time. Don't insist on an immediate, to the second, response to a request, but rather tolerate a little lag time while your child quickly, quietly, and probably benignly expresses his displeasure.

When your child saves face you will gain cooperation.

WHY IT WORKS

Whether it's a young child who is insisting that a puzzle goes together a certain way, or an older child who never gets invited to parties or who is insisting that he has no math assignment when it turns out he does, saving face will help him learn and move ahead. Instead of getting stuck in an angry and resentful place where he will expend way too much negative energy proving himself, you will be helping him use his powers constructively.

Younger children are trying to master as much as they can, and if their egos are developing on track, are fairly sure they can do much more than they actually can. Sometimes this can be dangerous, other times funny, and still others, extremely frustrating for everyone involved. If you fight to the end they will likely revert into tantrum behavior. You are forcing your child to give up his quest, his most heartfelt desire. To do for himself. But by giving him a little space to "stand tall" you will be letting him know you want him to grow also. He will not experience defeat, which in turn will help him release his clutch on an obstinate stand you cannot allow.

When it comes to an older child, by allowing him some room to make a wrong move or have a problem without you jumping all over it, you've showed him that you do not wish to control his every move. He has a right to his feelings, and his independent beliefs, even when they don't agree with yours, or prove to be incorrect are okay with you.

Also, by not placing yourself on a pedestal as the one who knows everything while he is just a foolish child, you do not diminish or humiliate him. You allow him to respect his mistake because you understand his reasons for making it.

As a result, your child will walk away from the situation with his ego intact, and with less anger, most of which will then disappear shortly after the encounter. Also, had you pushed him too far, he would have approached the next confrontation with an even fiercer drive to prove himself.

THE DEEPER MESSAGE

Many children are easily humiliated.

They are all, at any age, struggling to separate from their parents, and to prove to themselves and you that they can move out into the world with skill, intelligence, and strength. But at the same time they are afraid they can't, or that you won't let them, or that they really don't want to, or that they'll fail.

When you back a child into the corner, when you say, "I want it THIS SECOND," or "I knew you were wrong," or "How come none of your friends call here anymore?" his feeling of powerlessness will be profound. He will hear it as you saying, "You are not free. You do as I say. I am stronger and wiser and I notice you're not doing too well."

This feeling of powerlessness can turn into terrible shame and/or anger, neither of which you will want to nurture within your child.

However, by giving him a little room to navigate, you will be saying, "I know you're separate from me. That you have a right to hold some thoughts and feelings to yourself. That you think differently. That you can't move when I move. And that's okay. I think you are capable. But sometimes I think you might need help and lots of times I need you to follow my rules.''

This will build confidence. It will help him see that mistakes or weaknesses do not define a person. And that despite a misstep or two he can continue to positively forge ahead.

SEEING IT IN ACTION:

Your Four-Year-Old

Your four-year-old is struggling into a pair of jeans that has a difficult button at the waist. ''I can do it,'' he insists as his still-chubby fingers pull and push at the button opening. Nothing happens. You are growing impatient as you have to get him off to school.

''Here, let me help you,'' you say, reaching out to assist him.

''NO!'' he practically shrieks. ''I can do it!''

For an agonizing long minute you watch as he pushes, prods, and sweats to no avail. You can see he's growing more and more upset. His breathing is even coming in short little heaves.

''I'll tell you what,'' you offer calmly. ''I've seen you do lots of buttons. I know you can do it. But this one even I have trouble with. I remember that from last week. How about if I give it a try and you can do the zipper?''

Chances are he'll look up at you now filled with a mixture of self-disgust and defeat.

Repeat the part about it being hard as you do the button. "This IS tight," you might say. "That's why it's so hard to do!"

Then as he pulls up his zipper, smile at him and say something like, "I think we did that very well together!"

You made yourself his partner. You did not compare your skills. And you gave him some room to do something else for himself.

He may not feel victorious, but he won't feel demeaned either.

Your Eight-Year-Old

Your four-year-old daughter has been looking all over for her bright pink sparkling yo-yo. She asks your eight-year-old at least ten times, "Lauren, where's my yo-yo? Do you have my yo-yo?"

At first Lauren volunteers to look in her room. You notice she does a perfunctory job of it and then emerging a minute later announces, "I don't have it."

But your youngest is persistent, having torn apart the playroom and not having found it.

Lauren is now very irritated at being questioned. "I don't know where it is," she insists. "I don't have it."

Finally you decide to join the hunt. This yo-yo has become the holy grail and you're as curious as your younger daughter. In fact, you could swear you saw it in someone's bedroom just yesterday.

After rustling about in your youngest daughter's room you make your way into Lauren's. And in short order you find the yo-yo.

It's under Lauren's bed.

You promptly stand up and glance in Lauren's direction. She's busy straightening out her books. Something she never does.

"Honey, did you hide this?" you ask her softly.

"NO!" Lauren cries out. "I didn't. We were playing with our yo-yo's yesterday, and mine broke and I borrowed hers and then she played with it, too, and then . . . that's what happened."

The problem here, of course, is that you can't know exactly what happened. The truth may indeed be gray. Or it may not be. So, since you didn't see Lauren actively hide the yo-yo, all you can do now is try to turn this into a constructive moment. One that minimizes the chances of this happening again, and that encourages each child to develop a sense of responsibility.

"Well, I don't know why it's here," you might begin. "I can certainly understand why you'd want to play with hers if yours is broken, but surely you looked under your bed?"

Having given her a little understanding, she may admit she saw it there, or she may not.

If she doesn't, move on to part two.

"This is how I see it. This is your sister's toy. It's in your room. And if it's in your room, you have to be the one who's responsible for it being here. I'm not saying you hid it purposely. I'm simply saying you should be sure that her toys end up in her room just like she should check that yours end up in yours."

She'll probably nod at this, after which you can say something like, "In the future, though, please look a little harder when something is missing. Okay?"

Hiding a sibling's toy is a classic move. It's a little sneaky but temptation is so powerful . . . after all the toy is in the house and is often shared and so on and so forth

. . . that the most important thing is to point out how you want your children to sort out their belongings. Not that one or the other is a criminal.

Lauren's a little girl who needs to develop some impulse control. By letting her slip out of "getting caught" she will likely think twice before giving in to temptation again. You will have told her that you know she can behave honestly, and here's the rule to follow. By allowing her to save face, she did not get caught up defending herself.

Instead, you empowered her to find the control within.

Your Twelve-Year-Old

Your seventh grader walks in the door at three-thirty on Wednesday, and sits down for a snack.

"So," you ask, "do you have a lot of math homework today?"

"Don't have any," he responds in a garbled voice, mouth stuffed with cookies.

"You always have math homework on Wednesdays," you say with surprise. "How can that be?"

"We just don't have any," he insists. You can see his shoulders begin to tense. He looks up at you with annoyance. "She didn't give us any." He takes another bite. "I don't think."

At this point you're probably ready to rifle through his book bag to prove your point, or insist that he clearly doesn't know what he's talking about. But give him some room.

"Well, you don't sound absolutely positive to me. Why don't you give someone in your class a call to see if you do have any? It will only take a minute and it'll save you getting into trouble at school tomorrow."

He may shrug at this, unwilling to give up his position. It won't be out of laziness. The problem is he already went on record as saying he didn't have any. It's hard to back down and accept he might be wrong.

"Maybe you were working on a problem in class and you didn't hear her give the assignment," you might try evenly. "Things like that happen, you know."

Chances are at this point he'll make the call.

If you hear him say something like, "Oh really? Okay, what is it?" get busy doing something. Wipe off the counter, study something on the refrigerator, or simply leave the room for a moment.

Once he's off the phone, he may or may not say something to you. He'll probably either go the route of muttering, "I do have SOME math homework," or simply try to ease out of the kitchen without saying a word.

Whichever way he chooses, let him go without an "I told you so," or "Now, aren't you glad you called?" Both speak to your superiority.

You could say nothing. If that doesn't feel quite right, you might try, "Good! Now you'll be prepared tomorrow," or very matter-of-factly, "Let me know if you need any help."

Whatever happens don't expect an apology. That takes a level of maturity and confidence your son may not yet have. It takes a while for a person to realize that to say "I'm sorry. I was wrong," doesn't mean he's a fool.

TECHNIQUE #6

A TOUCH OF HUMOR

WORKS FOR: ANY SITUATION IN WHICH YOU TYPICALLY EXPRESS ANNOYANCE IN ORDER TO CHANGE BEHAVIOR SUCH AS A DIRTY ROOM, CHORES LEFT UNDONE, HOMEWORK INCOMPLETE—A WELL-CHOSEN MOMENT WHEN A CHILD HAS BEEN VERY UPSET.

THE TECHNIQUE

There are a few things everyone knows about telling jokes. When you tell a joke, timing is everything. It surprises listeners, it catches them off guard, and in so doing it makes them laugh. And, of course, you don't tell the same joke twice to the same person. Nor do you tell a joke to a person who is in deep distress.

The same is true here. You can't use humor too often in the same situation because it will lose its punch. Little will get accomplished. You also have to choose your moment carefully. Using humor or a light comment to diffuse a situation is something you have to feel your way through. Something you have to time well.

If your child's room is a mess every morning and you regularly impatiently announce, "Get this room neatened up now BEFORE breakfast," one morning try humor instead. "Oh, my," you might say as you survey the devastation. "How lovely. Can you get it just a little messier, though, honey. I mean I see a corner over there without a toy on it.'' Then smile gamely at your child and say, ''Clean it up, dear.'' Then simply walk out.

If your child is deeply upset about something you think is silly you might use humor, too, but not before you've given his feelings credence (see technique #5). Perhaps someone has told him he's dumb and he feels hurt. Let him know you think it was mean and you don't blame him for getting upset. Explain how people often accuse others of things they are most afraid of in themselves. Let that sink in and after you've patted his back a few times you might start humorously massaging his scalp. ''Just getting those brains supercharged for tomorrow!'' you might explain. And if your child is deeply distressed about something quite serious, humor (or a light comment) is only useful after she's calmed down and can be there with you. Perhaps she's the only one of her friends not to make the cheerleading team. After she's cried her eyes out and after you've discussed each angry or hurt thought, you might try saying something light such as, ''Look at it this way. You'll get to sit in the stands next to whatever cute guy you like, while they'll have to be on the field wondering what you're up to!''

However, when you use humor, watch your child carefully. Sometimes, depending on the age of your child or the situation with which she is coping, humor could be misunderstood and viewed as sarcasm, a taunt, or tease. If this happens, quickly explain what you were trying to do. ''I know you feel terrible, but I was just trying to show you that there is a kind of funny side to bad things sometimes.'' Then repeat, ''I don't think what you're upset about is funny.''

WHY IT WORKS

Humor works for different reasons in different situations. If you've gotten in the habit of screaming at your child for chores undone, a messy room, sloppy homework, or a flood on the bathroom floor, suddenly using humor will catch him off guard. Rather than spiraling into an argument that will only draw out the confrontation and build resentment, humor will usually leave everyone feeling more agreeable.

In other words, he won't be wrestling with you. He'll be left to wrestle with the task at hand.

In a situation where a small thing has gotten blown up way out of proportion, a little humor will bring it down to size and point up the ridiculousness of the problem.

Many children are inexperienced with feelings of deep hurt or grief. When there is a distressing situation, a touch of humor or a light comment will bring a child some relief from her own pain and keep her from feeling too much hopelessness or fear. Pain can be scary. Humor removes the edge.

THE DEEPER MESSAGE

You are modeling (see technique #6) a very important coping mechanism. Things can get very difficult in life. There are things we don't want to do but must do. There are things that hurt us. And there are things that are so painful it can feel as if we can't survive.

But a person can survive and you are displaying how humor can help. It can make a situation feel less intense, it can bring out a brighter side of life, and it can increase your ability to cope by halting, even if only for a brief moment, the onslaught of difficult thoughts and feelings.

By first paying serious attention to the pain of a situation you will be respecting your child's right to feel bad. But by using humor at a well-timed moment you will be showing your child that she can take some control over the situation and her own feelings. That even the darkest of moments can be pierced by light.

SEEING IT IN ACTION:

Your Four-Year-Old

Jack is the slowest eater on earth. Most of dinnertime is caught up with reminders, "Take another bite," or threats, "Jack, if you don't eat those peas right now there will be no dessert." By the time everyone has finished their meal you have indigestion, the pitch of your voice has risen markedly, and your son's plate has barely been touched. You're glaring at him and he's glaring at you.

Tonight, you are serving him macaroni and cheese, something you know he likes. The scene begins as before. Everyone starts eating and Jack stares down at his plate.

"Oh, Jack," you might try, "I forgot to tell you. Don't eat."

He looks at you curiously.

"Yes. Superman dropped in just a few minutes ago

and he put something really funny in your food and he said it would make you fly. But I don't want you to fly, so don't eat it." Smile nicely.

"He did not!" Jack will probably laugh.

"He did," you say evenly. "Don't eat. No flying around here. Uh-uh. No sir."

Jack will likely reach for his fork.

"Please don't." You can laugh now, letting him know you're being silly with him. "He said once you're through you'll be able to fly and I'm afraid you'll bump your head on the ceiling!"

Probably Jack will start eating. Slowly at first, just to join in the fun.

"Oh no!" you can periodically cry out. "What are we going to do? Your poor head!"

When the meal is over pick him up and fly him around the house for a moment or two, as a reward for his "playing along."

If you're in the mood, you can create another story the next night and a few nights after. Chances are you will be making great headway in breaking the dinnertime pattern.

However, if you're not in the mood, *don't do it*. Even a young child can tell if the spirit isn't there. Use humor when you can, and you'll be making sure that at least a few nights a week, he has a good meal and you digest your food.

Your Nine-Year-Old

Sam comes home from school extremely upset. Two kids had gotten together at school, and teased him about having a pig nose.

The truth is, it is a little wide at the base, but your son is a perfectly nice-looking boy and certainly nothing about his appearance should draw that kind of attention. He, however, doesn't seem to see things that way and very hurt, is now standing in the kitchen angrily opening and closing cabinets looking for something to eat.

"You do not have a pig nose, Sam," you begin. "But I know that doesn't much matter. If someone says something like that it hurts."

"I do look like a pig," Sam yells. "Otherwise they wouldn't have said that.

"That's not true. People say all sorts of stupid things to other people for one very important reason. They want to make others feel bad. Somehow if they can make someone else feel weak or hurt, it lets them feel stronger. 'Course that feeling doesn't last."

Sam shrugs. "I don't know."

"I do know," you say. You let him sit and ponder your observation for a little while.

"It's very unkind to make fun of people. You must be very angry." You pick up a magazine lying on the counter and turn to a political cartoon. There's a sketch of President Clinton with a huge bulbous nose.

"You think he looks like that in person?" you ask.

Your son smiles. "No."

"He doesn't. But he does have a broad tip on his nose so that the cartoonist exaggerated it like crazy."

Smiling, you take a piece of paper and say, "I think my eyes are too close." You draw a picture of yourself with eyes practically on your nose. "There." You grin. "That's me"

"No it isn't." Your son laughs. Then he quickly grows somber. "I hate Jimmy and Greg."

The time for humor is over. You don't push. You used it to get a point across but now it's time to stop.

"Well, who knows what a cartoonist would do if they saw Jimmy and Greg." You smile.

"Probably give Jimmy huge ears," your son replies. He breaks out into a smile once more.

Your Twelve-Year-Old

This is the evening of your daughter Tina's first dance and with great trepidation you wait for her to return home. She went off looking adorable but she's a little behind her friends in physical development and you're afraid she may not receive much attention from the boys.

Sure enough around the time that she is due home, you hear the front door slam and feet pounding up the stairs. Moments later Tina throws open your bedroom door and with tears streaming down her face, cries out, "No one asked me to dance!"

She throws herself down on your bed between you and her father and sobs her heart out. Neither of you say a word. You just stroke her hair.

"I'll never get a boyfriend," she manages to choke out. "I'm so ugly . . ."

"That's not true," you and your husband say softly, over and over.

Finally, when she's calmed down you ask her to look at you, which she does.

"You look a little younger than your friends right now. That's going to change *very* soon. I have a feeling that might be why this happened tonight. You're going to have to be patient."

"You are going to be beautiful," her father says confidently.

"I'm not . . ." your daughter replies.

"Like an angel . . ." you say dreamily, going for a laugh.

"Stop it," your daughter says angrily. "That's not true."

She's right. It isn't true, though Tina is certainly attractive, and right now what you said isn't funny. First you'd been up-front and honest and then seconds later you'd gone off into LaLa Land. It felt like a jab.

"You're right. I was just trying to be funny at the wrong time. What happened tonight is painful and I'm not so sure I would have found what I said so funny either if I were you."

Your daughter nods and sniffles. "That's okay."

"But you know, honey, someday someone is going to think you look like an angel, even if you don't. Because that someone's going to love you. . . ."

She shrugs and nods thoughtfully.

TECHNIQUE #7

READ MY LIPS

WORKS FOR: ANY SITUATION IN WHICH YOU WANT WHAT YOU HAVE JUST SAID, REQUESTED, DEMANDED, OR DECIDED TO BE TAKEN UTTERLY AND COMPLETELY SERIOUSLY.

THE TECHNIQUE

First, you must determine how you really feel—not how you assume another parent might react, or what the books say—but what you deeply think is important. No words can be spoken with true conviction, unless you know deeply where you stand.

Then it is absolutely critical that you not only say what you mean, but look and sound the part. Firm words interrupted by an ambivalent smile or sigh won't work. Neither will an angry voice. Angry voices carry too much emotion and will overwhelm the message.

You need to say what you expect *and feel* in a matter-of-fact, determined voice, looking straight at your child with a look of complete conviction. And without smiling immediately afterward. (A smile is often used after a confrontation as if to say, ''Please don't be mad at me.'' This only results in being taken half seriously.)

If part of what you are saying involves a consequence and you are feeling intensely angry or frustrated, it is a good idea to refrain from laying one out at that moment. Simply say, "You will receive a consequence for this but I want to sort one out that makes sense. I'll discuss it with you in a little while." (See technique #1.) In this way, as discussed earlier, you will avoid bursting forth with a punishment ("You are grounded for a month!") you couldn't really mean. Of course, if you do announce a consequence firmly and convincingly, which you realize later is unfair, you can back off.

But you need to do so in a very particular way. Many parents, upset with themselves for overdoing it, announce, "Well, I think I was a little harsh. You can watch TV after tonight," even if it's only been one day so far! Rather, you need to make it clear that you think a consequence of some significance is in order and that even though you may have gone too far, it doesn't mean you can forget the whole thing.

"I think no TV for three weeks was a little harsh. I was very angry when I said it. I think one week is sufficient."

What if you've been waffling over every issue and need to change that pattern? If you're a parent who has been waffling over most matters, don't try to stand firm on absolutely everything at once. Both you and your child will be overwhelmed and will likely find yourselves relentlessly locked in battle. Actually, even one issue over which you have been waffling, will be difficult to address. Expect rebellion until your child sees you really mean it. Then attack each issue methodically and separately.

As a last point on technique, there are many parents hampered by the idea that one should reason with one's child. Explain everything. Look at nuance as much as possible.

But sometimes that just isn't so. Sometimes negotiations just muddle the facts. Sometimes, something just has to be, and that's it . . . no matter how anyone feels.

And that's what this technique is about. Having the courage and conviction to say, "Listen to me. I mean this. It may hurt. It may not seem fair. But now, there's is no discussion."

WHY IT WORKS

It will work because your child will *know* how you feel. He won't question it, because you aren't. He won't try to sidestep it (more than once) because he will learn to recognize that when you speak like this you stand behind your words, with feelings. And it will work because no child likes to be in too much control.

Children of every age have impulses that frighten them. There are so many things they want, so many temptations, so many pressures, and so much to explore but always there is the vague awareness that mixed into all that glitters is a danger zone. Dangers from outside (getting into trouble) and dangers from within (somehow exploding from the mixture of excitement and anxiety if everything were to become available). Standing firm will take the full responsibility of self-control away from your child, until as an adult he is better able to pace himself. Your child needs this, and deep down he knows it, too.

THE DEEPER MESSAGE

It is important (and helpful) to realize that connection takes place during friction and limit setting. No matter how much a child may rail against your words, the sense of being "held" and "guarded" will keep her feeling anchored. Also, a parent who continually gives in to a child's desires is failing to help her gain the ability to cope with disappointment, sadness, and frustration. She will gain a distorted sense of what real life is like; some situations make it impossible to have things the way one would like them. She may also develop an inability to follow directions in school and the workplace, as well as a reluctance to be generous with friends. By holding the line, a parent is teaching a child about the realities of life. No one can have everything. No one can do everything. No one can feel fulfilled every moment. But a person can still feel satisfied and happy even without the whole world at her beck and call.

SEEING IT IN ACTION:

Your Four-Year-Old

You have just gotten a new dining-room table and your son is running about the room flailing a hard plastic sword. He's just seen a cartoon of King Arthur and this new piece of furniture has become his round table. You are pleased at his active imagination, but feeling very uptight about the table. It was expensive, you've wanted a new one for quite some time, and even though you're charmed by your son's ability to transform an oblong wood slab into a circle surrounded by knights arguing over which dragon to slay, you are becoming increasingly more annoyed. Not to mention torn.

Heaven forbid you should squelch his creativity.

And so you pause. How do you really feel? The truth is you want this table safe and there are many other rooms in the house with a table. Like the kitchen for instance. Or the coffee table that is already old and scratched. And so you make up your mind.

You begin with a mix of playfulness (he *is* young) and firmness.

"King Arthur, stop hitting the table with your sword right now. It's new and I don't want it to get any scratches. Please call your knights into the kitchen."

"No! No!" he cries out. "This is my kingdom," he adds, swinging the sword about to indicate the length and breadth of his domain.

So the time for playfulness is just about over.

"I'm afraid this dining room is *my* kingdom," you say firmly. "Yours is in the kitchen. Or the den where I believe there is a knight or two already waiting."

"But . . ."

"Andy, leave the dining room now," you finally say firmly. "Leave now or you will have to give me your sword, which I will put away until tomorrow." You are bending down to look him straight in the eyes, one hand protectively on the table. "This table means a lot to me. I do not want it scratched or harmed in any way. Do you understand?"

"Yeah . . ." Andy replies, heading out of the dining room. And he does, too. Because you didn't change your message for one minute. ''Come on, Knight James,'' he calls over his shoulder. ''Let's go to the *real* table.''

Your Eight-Year-Old

Adam, your eight-year-old has had it with his four-year-old brother Jason. He wants his toys left alone. He wants him out of his room most of the time. And he wants to push him every time they pass in the hall. In some ways you can't blame him. Jason can't keep his hands off anything that doesn't belong to him. Still, you've told Adam repeatedly to stop pushing Jason. He doesn't listen. His frustration gets the better of him.

This last time, however, Adam believing his younger brother ''stole'' a missing Z-BOT, pushes him so hard that Jason trips and falls.

''That's it,'' you cry out angrily. ''I've had it. I've told you over and over to stop pushing your brother and you don't listen and now you've really hurt him!'' All the while you're cradling Jason in your arms who isn't seriously harmed but is certainly enjoying the drama of his own wrenching sobs.

''Well, I didn't mean to push him so hard but he took my Z-BOT!'' Adam cries out indignantly. ''He deserves it.''

''Nobody in this house deserves getting pushed,'' you yell back at him. ''NOBODY.'' You can feel yourself spinning out of control.

''Well, he does,'' Adam insists.

''You are not allowed to touch your brother ever again,'' you plow forward, getting this uncomfortable feeling you're about to say something even more ridiculous like, ''I'm going to take every Z-BOT you own along with their vehicles and give them away to needy children today. Help me pack them up right now.''

But instead, you take a deep breath and say, ''I'm very angry. It is not acceptable for you to mistreat your brother like this and you are going to have to have a consequence. But I don't want to figure out what that is right now because I'm too upset to think clearly. In the meantime, please go to your room.''

You take a long hot bubble bath and feel yourself calming down. About an hour later you go up to your son's room. ''The consequence will be I am taking your Z-BOTS away for twenty-four hours. I will explain to your brother, however, that he is not to go near the toys in your room under any circumstances.''

''But that's not . . . !'' your son starts to protest.

''It's fair. We don't hurt people in this house. Nor, I admit, do we take things that don't belong to us, not that we even know *if* your brother took your toy this time. At any rate, that's the consequence and I suggest you get busy reading a book or doing a puzzle, because arguing with me will get you nowhere.''

You will have made it clear you mean business, that you are trying to be fair, and that his time is better spent on other things.

Your Twelve-Year-Old

Your sixth grader calls from a friend's house a few minutes before she's due home from school.

''Hi, Mom! I know I'm supposed to come right home after school and get my homework done, but can I stay and get it done with Julie?''

This is not, you realize, an unreasonable request, except that past experience has taught you again and again that when your daughter "gets homework done" at a friend's she's really just sitting there with her notebook open, talking about boys.

"Sorry, honey," you reply evenly. "Come home now and get it done. When you're through you can call Julie and talk a while."

"But that's so stupid! So unfair!" your daughter yelps. "How could you be like that!?"

"It's not hard," you say mildly. "I realize I'm not perfect, but despite that I insist. You come home now."

"But I could get everything done. . . ."

"Come home now," you repeat flatly. There's no point reminding her that her work never gets done when she's at a friend. She'll only retort, "But this time will be different!"

And, of course, you can't prove that it won't be.

Remember, there's a time for negotiation. And there's a time for a benign dictatorship.

"I hate you," your daughter hisses.

"You're angry at me," you acknowledge. "Please come home."

She hangs up.

And she's home about ten minutes later.

Filled with indignation she stomps upstairs without an "hello" and proceeds to do her work.

You call her down for dinner two hours later.

She appears quiet but not exactly hostile.

By the end of the meal she's downright friendly.

Why?

Because somewhere inside she knew the work would not get done . . . or at least not in the same way it did once she was alone.

Because the limits resulted in her doing a job she's proud of.

Because you didn't confuse her. She heard you. She did it.

The situation was out of her hands.

In a way, it was a relief.

TECHNIQUE #8

WHEN HE'S DONE SOMETHING WRONG, LEAD WITH HIS STRENGTH

WORKS FOR: LYING—HURTING SOMEONE'S FEELINGS—RUDENESS—CHEATING—STEALING—BREAKING SOMETHING—TERRIBLE GRADES—FAILING A TEST—DOING SOMETHING DANGEROUS—HITTING SOMEONE—ACTING IRRESPONSIBLY IN ANY WAY.

THE TECHNIQUE

Begin your talk by communicating your belief in your child's basic goodness. ''I know that you are an honest person. I've seen that in many of the things you say and do. You must feel terrible that you lied today.''

Then try and draw him out. Express your interest in what was going on for him. Why would he behave in such an unusual way? Was there a particular reason that he told the lie? Make it clear you are very interested and concerned about the difficult feelings he must have had that inspired him to lie.

After you have talked it through as well as you can, make it clear that no matter what the reasons, lying is wrong and that there is going to have to be a consequence. You can either name one yourself or ask him to contribute (see technique #1).

As always, try and keep the punishment related to the infraction, or at least proportionate.

For a younger child, a consequence is not often going to be as effective as finding a resolution to the problem at hand. He is only just beginning to develop his sense of right and wrong and so a consequence would only be seen as a harsh punishment for an unclear reason. Turning an undesirable behavior into a desirable one will be much more effective. If he's throwing little beads around his room and crying out "It's raining," tell him that looks like fun but that it's going to be awfully hard to find all the beads. Pick some of them up to prove your point, then take him outside and encourage him to do the same with leaves or acorns.

WHY IT WORKS

Leading with something positive will help to minimize your child's defensive position. He knows he's done something wrong, that you are angry, and that he deserves to be punished. He probably feels quite remorseful. But he doesn't like this state of affairs at all, and is likely to be very guarded, waiting for a "fight."

You will want to almost literally disarm him.

Compassion is a wonderful tool and speaks to the fact that you are both thinking, feeling people. An event happened. A person whom you *both* care about was behind it. By speaking to your child in an available, supportive way you will help him to open up.

Certainly he should feel some responsibility, and if appropriate, guilt. It will help him control his impulses.

But you will want him to limit that guilt to a particular situation. Too sweeping a criticism could all too easily leave him believing, "I'm a terrible person."

As for a consequence, all the understanding in the world does not negate the need for one. Your child, in fact, will likely feel better if he gets one. It will in many ways alleviate his conscience. It's not just a question of righting the wrong, which is often impossible. (Of course if that is doable, that, too, should be explored.) It's about underlining the significance of the mistake.

Also, a child needs to know that a parent is prepared to set limits. On the one hand, she might wish she could do anything, but that degree of freedom is also frightening and overwhelming. Where, after all, does she stop? And why? And does anyone care?

The consequence proves you're watching. You care. You want to make a point. You want your child to think and remember. And she will. Because first, you made her feel understood.

In terms of the younger child, by changing his behavior from one that is difficult to one that works, you are building his ability to control his impulses and to see there are many ways to accomplish a task or satisfy a whim.

But most importantly, this technique works because in moving past the event itself, you reduce the chances of a repeat performance. By not concentrating so much on how wrong it was, and how could he have done it, you will be talking instead about how much faith you have in your child and how much you want to understand what was going on for him at the time. You may uncover some problems related to peer influence or a fear your child harbors that you knew nothing about. The ensuing conversation will help to ensure your child will not behave this way again.

Leading with her strength will enable your child to have that conversation in a more open and useful way.

THE DEEPER MESSAGE

It is important always to communicate to your child that a person can do a bad thing and still be a good and valued person who respects herself. It is also critical to let her know that you value how she feels more than what she's done. That the problems or issues that lead to the mistake are more significant to you than her mistake. This message will go a long way toward establishing a trusting relationship filled with goodwill.

The consequence, however, will tell your child that while her feelings and motivations matter, you are going to keep her anchored in the real world. She can count on you to make judgment calls that make sense, that consider her, but that also address your expectations of her.

By approaching her mistake with compassion you will be telling your child, "I know you can do better. I'll help you do that if you need me to. But you are a responsible, strong person who can own up to what you've done. That takes character."

And in so doing, you will be helping to create character, conscience, and a value system inside your child. It will aid her considerably in developing her own clear sense of right and wrong.

SEEING IT IN ACTION:

Your Four-Year-Old

You have just found your four-year-old child perched on the precarious top shelf of your closet, having gotten there by dragging a chair over to your dresser, climbing on top of that, and somehow pulling himself up. He is rooting around through your scarves, one of which is now dangling over his head.

Even if you know he knows better, having been caught in similar circumstances before, calmly walk over, stretch out your hands and firmly say, "Pete, come down from there right now. It's very dangerous. That shelf could break any minute."

Once you have him down and safe and are staring into his apprehensive face, begin by saying, "I know those scarves are tempting. You like to play with them and I can't say I blame you for that."

He'll likely nod and say with great relief, something like, "Yes. 'Cause then I can pretend I'm a bandit . . ." Chances are he knew something about being in that closet wasn't quite right.

"Okay," you might answer, "but I have two things to say. One, those scarves belong to Mommy. You have other things to play with so that you can be a bandit. And two, you are not allowed to climb on my closet shelves. You could get very hurt."

He may nod or shrug at this and so you will go on. "You need to think of some ways for you to be a bandit that don't have anything to do with my scarves. Why don't you go in your room now and see how many things you can find that would help you look just like one?''

And then, if you'd like, go with him. Once he's all decked out you can gently say, ''You see? Next time you are tempted to do something dangerous like climb in my closet to be a bandit, think of something you know is okay instead.''

By following this technique you will have let your child feel understood, warned, and clever at the same time.

Your Eight-Year-Old

You received a call earlier in the afternoon from school that your eight-year-old angrily hit the child at the adjacent desk over the head with a book. The teacher commented that your daughter has lately been getting into a number of arguments with two particular children in the class, but she isn't sure why.

Your child is now walking in the door as if nothing happened.

You offer her a snack and then sit down at the table with your daughter. You begin with the facts.

''I got a call from school today. Your teacher told me you hit Jane over the head with a book.''

''She made me mad,'' your daughter might reply, not sure yet if she's in trouble or not. After all, you don't look angry.

''I guess she did because usually you don't do things like that. You talk about what gets you angry, which is wonderful.''

''She told me I can't read as fast as she can. I got really mad. It's not true exactly,'' she replies angrily.

"It must not have felt very good hitting her, though."

She shrugs. Or she may look up at you tearfully.

"What's going on, honey? Are you upset about your reading?"

Try and draw her out as much as possible. Is the reading the problem? Have a few kids been ganging up on her? Is she being teased in school? This is an opportunity not only to find out what she might be holding back, but also to express your concern about her feelings of inadequacy in the classroom.

Then, of course, you have to get around to what she did. But even that can be posed in an understanding way.

"I think you are having trouble lately controlling yourself when you feel hurt or upset. You are going to have to work on that. No matter how you feel there is no excuse for hitting someone. You have to tell Jane to stop teasing you or ask your teacher to step in."

In terms of consequences, it is likely that your child has already received one from the teacher so you might want to refrain. But in another circumstance, such as hitting a child during a play date, do extend an immediate consequence. After, that is, you've extended your child some respect in front of his friend. "Peter should not have told you that you are a terrible batter. Peter, that was mean and unnecessary. Charlie, I don't blame you for getting mad. But please go in the house for three minutes and calm yourself down. Hitting is just not allowed."

Charlie will understand you're on his side. He might even be glad for the chance to separate from Peter. He probably still wants to hit him and needs a little help with impulse control.

Your Twelve-Year-Old

Your twelve-year-old was caught copying off the paper of the girl sitting next to her during a math test. She has brought a note home from the teacher and is standing before you now somewhat defiantly. "Here" she says, "I wasn't cheating. I was just checking!"

Chances are, if your daughter was caught copying off someone's paper, she was cheating. And in any event even checking is cheating. This does not, however, mean your child is dishonest or lazy. Cheating often happens because kids are simply afraid not to. And, in fact, other rather significant infractions are also more a reflection of an important yet benign problem than a pathological one. Tarring and feathering won't help a thing. Nor will the reflex fear that something is dreadfully "wrong" with your child.

"You must have felt very embarrassed," you might begin, looking at your child sympathetically. "I know you know cheating, or as you say, "checking" isn't right. You're supposed to keep your eyes on your own paper."

"I didn't feel so bad," she insists unconvincingly.

"Well, I imagine you were looking at your neighbor's paper because you were worried about your own. Isn't that so? That's not a good feeling."

By now your child will probably relax her defiant stance a bit, and might even nod.

"So why were you so unsure about your own work, honey?" you ask.

Again, try and draw out why she was cheating, what she's afraid of if she does badly, and how you could possibly help to make her feel more confident.

Finally, if this is a second episode of cheating (the likely zero she received at school the first time would suffice), say that you are going to have to give her a consequence. Cheating is just not acceptable. But don't go overboard. If you can remember that cheating is not necessarily the actions of a nefarious mind, but rather a frightened, insecure adolescent, you will arrive at a just dessert. No TV for a week, or no going out after school tomorrow would be fine.

There is no point making a child feel like a criminal. She isn't. She's a good kid who made a bad choice for reasons you and she need to work on together. To rip her apart would only be to add to the embarrassing blow she has already received. She was most probably publicly told to hand in her paper. Kids were watching.

But suppose her infraction was breaking into a boarded-up house with her friends. You know she's not a risk taker and yet here she is, having just been dropped off by the local policeman. What then? You would want to know why. Did she get talked into it? How come she couldn't stand her ground?

Your most important job is to find out the whys and to let her know you realize she is basically an honest, good, trustworthy person. It will help develop her conscience, sense of personal strength, and give her some perspective on her own misstep.

Even though she may need a tutor!

WHOSE DREAM IS IT ANYWAY?

WORKS FOR: ANYTIME YOUR CHILD PURSUES AN ACTIVITY UNENTHUSIASTICALLY OR RESENTFULLY, AND YOU FIND YOURSELF INSISTING AND PUSHING—ANYTIME YOUR CHILD KEEPS PUSHING HIMSELF HARDER AND HARDER TO DO BETTER AT SOMETHING BUT APPEARS TO EXPERIENCE NO ENJOYMENT.

THE TECHNIQUE

It is critical to recognize the difference between giving your child a chance to experiment with various activities in order to find what most interests her, and foisting your own dreams upon her.

In order to see the situation with some clarity, pay close attention to your own level of interest and emotional response to your child's pursuits. Regularly ask yourself the questions, "Am I enjoying this more than him?" "Why am I feeling so upset at his disinterest?" "Why do I feel so invested in her doing well?" and perhaps most importantly "Is this something I had wanted for me?" Reality check your reactions with other people.

Whether your son is playing football or chess, your daughter playing soccer or piano, if in response to a lack of enthusiasm, or a weakness in your child's performance you become distressed and overly involved, it is very likely this activity is more for you than him.

In order for your child to enjoy who he is and what he does, it has to come from him. You can encourage. But there is a difference between encouraging and pushing. And the clearest way to know which you are doing, is by honestly assessing the level of your own emotional response.

If your daughter who is a good swimmer doesn't like swim meets, and you think she should just finish out the year and then choose another sport next year, you're probably not pushing. If it hurts and frustrates you that she doesn't put her all into a race, it's probably your dream that's in the slow lane, not hers.

This technique is about listening to your child and monitoring your own reactions. It's about recognizing that your child has a right to feel attracted to the pursuits he feels are most comfortable and satisfying to him, no matter what you might have wished for him. And it's very much about saying and meaning, "What do *you* want to do?"—both to yourself and your child.

Often, when a parent pushes hard for a child's success it has to do with the parent's own frustrated ambition. While you're trying to help your child find herself, it might be a good idea for you to think about your own unexplored dreams for yourself. If you can experience a success that belongs to you, it will be that much easier to let your child find one that belongs to her.

WHY IT WORKS

You will want your child to enjoy what he is pursuing. The only way this will happen is if he's doing it for him.

If it's your dream, and he's doing it for you, a number

of things could happen. A tremendous tension could build between you. He might push himself too hard, in an effort to please you. He may achieve great success or failure but either way it won't be good. Anxiety will reign. If he does beautifully he may begin to believe this is why you love him. If he does poorly he may begin to feel that he isn't good enough for you.

A child who is introduced to activities in a manner that says, "Here, try this. I want you to broaden your horizons. Keep at it for a little while, and if it doesn't interest you we'll try something else," will do far better than one who senses the message is, "This is a great activity. It would give me such a kick to see you really do it. If you keep at it I know you'll love it."

And what does "do far better" mean? It means you will have a child who does not resent you. He will feel respected and happily experiment with activities, knowing if it's not his cup of tea, that's okay. He will want to please himself and will more confidently approach a new activity knowing it's not a trap. And he will not question his ability to keep your love.

THE DEEPER MESSAGE

You and your child are separate people. You should not need her to realize your dreams, to give you a thrill, or to do something in particular that makes you proud. Nor should she have to take care of you emotionally. You have your own life in which you pursue activities that excite you and give you a sense of self-worth. You shouldn't need her for that. You only wish the same thing for her.

As a result of keeping your dreams separate, when it comes to seeking your approval your daughter will keep her eye on the issues that most matter—the values that you have tried to impart and not the degree of accomplishment she has achieved.

It's not how good she is. It's who she is.

SEEING IT IN ACTION:

Your Nine-Year-Old

Your mother was an incredible runner. Your brother was captain of his high school basketball team. And you used to play a mean game of tennis. But you let it slide, as a result of your hectic schedule, not to mention the fact that your game had been slipping because of it.

Your husband was never one for sports, however, and your son does not seem to be, either.

Still, you can't imagine why he shouldn't learn to play a decent game of tennis. After all, it's such a social game, and it will stand him in good stead when he's older and needing to associate on several levels with business colleagues.

And so you sign him up for lessons, to which he begrudgingly agrees. "All right," he remarks. "But not a baseball team."

You agree. He seems to hate team sports. You tell yourself that this is fine. You're being flexible, after all.

Zac begins the tennis lessons and as you are filled with interest, you pull up a chair and watch every moment. After each lesson you comment encouragingly, and then suggest he might like to hit a few balls with you. "No, thanks," he says matter-of-factly.

This continues throughout the semester. Zac dutifully takes the court, hits pretty well, but when he walks off the court there's no spark. He seems, in fact, bored.

Finally the set of lessons are over and you comment it's time to sign up for more.

"I don't really want to," he says quietly.

"Why?" you ask. "You're doing well."

"Because I don't much like tennis."

You can feel yourself tensing. Boys who can play a sport get along better with other boys, you think to yourself. What if people make fun of him? What's he going to do when he's a lawyer and it's a company outing and he doesn't play? Also, he needs some exercise.

Realizing you are feeling highly emotional, you don't insist on the spot. Silently, in a brooding mode, the two of you drive home. Zac gets out of the car the moment you pull in the driveway, and goes straight upstairs.

When your husband comes home, he listens to the story and then shakes his head at you. "Good lawyers have good careers because they're good at what they do. I agree he needs exercise but why don't we just make that clear and let him pick something that will give him just that? You've got to stop foisting your stereotypical jock ideas on your son."

You'd protest but you know he's right.

Later that evening, the two of you sit Zac down and tell him it's important to pick some form of physical activity. It's good for him emotionally and physically. You suggest a number of them, all of which he rejects.

Then, eyes up at the ceiling, he says, "What about

T'ai Chi? I saw something about that on TV that looked good.''

You're about to argue. It's so offbeat, after all.

But your husband loudly and quickly responds, "Sounds good. It's excellent for developing concentration skills." He smiles at you. "Every lawyer needs that."

You smile. The next day you try on a tennis dress that's been hanging in your closet unused for the last five years.

It still fits.

YOU CAN LEAD A CHILD TO WATER, BUT THEN . . .

WORKS FOR: KIDS WHO DON'T LIKE TO TRY NEW THINGS (FOOD, SPORTS, GAMES)—CAN'T COMMIT TO ANY ACTIVITY—STUBBORNLY REFUSE TO DO SOMETHING YOU WANT THEM TO DO.

THE TECHNIQUE

Once you've established that the activity or responsibility you want your child to take on, is not one that addresses your dreams and expectations (see technique #9), then it may be time to take action that either gives *both* of you room to maneuver, or simply and matter-of-factly "lays down the law."

But before you do anything, keep in mind that while you may not be inflicting your own personal frustrations or dreams on your child, you may still be creating expectations that are too high. Your child may not be developmentally or temperamentally capable of the task at hand, as you have set it out. This is a time to take a long, hard look at the child before you. Is she developmentally ready to read? Is he old (and big) enough to take out the garbage on his own? Is it fair to expect her to know, at her age, what she's doing when she commits to a year's worth of piano lessons?

A lot of these questions will have to be answered with your particular child in mind. And through checking with others and a little good, honest self-talk. Just because your daughter's best friend can sit and play the flute for two hours each day, doesn't mean Lisa should be ready to do the same.

Also, you may want to stop and evaluate if the issue is worth a power play. Not that power plays should be avoided. Sometimes they can't be. But you will want to pick and choose. Certainly trying a little humor or a small reward to get somewhere is fine, such as when you tell your child, "Okay. The rule is one new food a week. And each time you try, you get an extra cookie." But if this doesn't get you what you want, you may want to stop and think if it's such a critical issue anyway.

However, once you've established that the issue at hand is fair, realistic, and important, and your child is highly reluctant to see things your way, whether it's a new food, clarinet lessons, joining the baseball team, or going to Sunday school, follow this formula:

- Ask what she doesn't like or is afraid of.
- Acknowledge there may be some truth to her fears or concerns but that it is your firm belief that she cannot continually turn away from things of which she is not sure or familiar or seemingly disinterested.
- Insist that your child give whatever it is a try, but include a verbal contract that addresses the reasoning behind your position, and some wording that acknowledges her feelings. You may also want to add a positive incentive (see technique #11).

"Try the clarinet lessons for six months. You

have to give yourself a chance to gain some skill, before you will know if you like it or not, or if it's even the right instrument for you.'' ''You've only played with the baseball team two games. I recognize you're not the best player, but you committed yourself. You're part of a team. Finish out at least half the season, that's six more games, and then let's see where you're at. You may feel better about the game when you've had more practice. If you still hate it, you can quit.''

- Make it clear you are not concerned with how good she is at something. You want her to try, of course, but you don't care that she be ''the best.'' You simply want her to broaden her experiences and understand that commitments have to be honored.

- If there is no room for negotiation, if this is one time when you must assert your parental authority, then don't waffle. Do it. ''Sunday school is very important. You are going to complete your study there. If you refuse to go in a reasonable manner, if I have to fight with you tooth and nail each morning, there will be a consequence.'' And then, deliver on your promise. However, be sure he makes it to Sunday school. The consequence is *not* a trade-off for not doing something. It's a price for doing it in a way that makes *your* life extremely unpleasant.

WHY IT WORKS

First and foremost no one likes to be told what to do. But very often beneath a child's refusal to try something, or inability to stick with something, is a fear of the unknown or failure. Or it might be an issue of temperament.

By the very act of attempting to address the issues, you are letting your child know you do not simply want to stand there and "boss him around." You are interested in what's going on for him.

When you acknowledge that the food may, indeed, not taste good, or the piano may not be "her" instrument, you're taking the notion out of the shadows and into broad daylight where it will take on more realistic dimensions. "You're right. You may not like it. So you'll spit it out. But if you do like it, won't that be cool?" "It may turn out that the piano is not your thing. The world isn't going to end."

Finally, by attaching carefully chosen parameters to a situation, you are making it clear that both you and your child are going to have to give a little. You are not trying to get him to "march" to your drummer. You are allowing for the importance of *his* experience with an activity you have deemed important.

As for the situation where there is no room for compromise, and an understanding conversation does no good, the consequence will send the bottom line message. "I insist you do this. I am your parent, and I am asserting my right to guide you in a way I feel is important, even if you don't agree."

Your child won't like it. But if you don't take this stand too often, chances are after one consequence (he'll want to test the waters) he'll reluctantly do as you say. It will work, basically because he will have no choice.

THE DEEPER MESSAGE

You're not trying to boss your child around. But you do believe in your right to insist on certain things. You will not do so in a vacuum. You will respect how your child feels, but you believe for reasons you are willing to share, that there is something important at stake here, and whether she sees it or not, you will remain firm. While this may annoy your child, on another level she will appreciate that there are some guidelines she must follow. She is not going to be left to her sometimes confusing reactions. She is not going to have to parent herself. Some children, in fact, might even appreciate the push. Your son may be quite anxious to stay on the baseball team, but just too scared to keep it up. His anger at you as he stomps off to the field, could be just a cover-up for his own deep desire to do well and his fear that he won't.

And in terms of keeping at something you will have taught your child an important lesson. Any activity that's worth doing can present challenges. If you run from them each time the going gets rough, you'll accomplish nothing. Once your child weathers the storm, and comes out the other end, he will have learned something extraordinarily important about life.

SEEING IT IN ACTION:

Your Four-Year-Old

It is, you've decided, time for your four-year-old son Zac to learn how to read. It's the spring before kindergarten. He loves books, and his best friend can already recognize many words.

And so you sit him down, "Come here, buddy, let's look at this book!" you suggest.

"Okay," he gleefully replies, unaware that there's a task at hand. "Oh!" he exclaims. "It's a new book!"

He's right, of course. It's a special beginner reader.

"So," you say cheerily, "Let's see. This is a book about a puppy. See?" you say, pointing to the word. "PUP-PY"

Zac nods, staring intently at the page.

This pleases you. "And this word," you continue, "is BARKS."

Zac looks up at you curiously. "Daddy. I don't like words like that. Not that way. Read it to me . . ."

"But, Zac," you reply, immediately feeling yourself growing tense, "Wouldn't you like to learn to read?"

"No," he replies matter-of-factly. He smacks the book with his hand. "I don't like this book!"

"But, honey, if you could read there are so many . . ."

Zac is very agitated now. He loves books. But this is different. "I'm going to draw something," he mutters as he slips off your lap.

You watch him for a moment feeling disappointed. Then you begin to worry that if you insist on him reading, when he isn't ready, you might turn him off to books. You launch into some self-talk.

Zac may not be ready to read. Lots of kids his age aren't. He might do better learning with other kids around him. Isn't it better to simply allow him to enjoy books the way he knows how right now? you ask yourself.

What difference does it make if his friend Max can read? It's not like Zac's going to reach the age of twenty-one and be illiterate.

Quickly you pick up one of his favorite books and hold it up. "Okay! Story time!! Want me to read your very favorite? You don't have to learn to read right now. You can do that some other time." And then you smile.

Zac looks up from his drawing warily, but spotting the book, happily climbs onto your lap.

"You . . ." he says, as if to make sure you both understand each other ". . . do it."

Your Nine-Year-Old

Your nine-year-old daughter Jessie can't commit to anything. She tried soccer but dropped off the team after a few weeks. She enrolled in art class but after a few sessions decided it was boring. Piano lessons didn't last long and neither did drama class. Now she's taking flute lessons and already she's starting to make comments about how it's "too hard."

You've been trying to be patient. You don't want to push. You think she's very musical, but if she doesn't want to take lessons you've decided not to make a big deal about it. The problem is she has to learn to stick with something.

It's not a question of your dreams for her. You know this because you don't care what she chooses, so long as she works through whatever stands in the way of her really enjoying something.

So you sit her down.

"This has to stop," you say firmly. "I don't care what you choose or how good or bad you are at it, you need to find an outside interest and stick with it long enough to get some rewards."

"I just want to hang out with my friends," she replies stubbornly. "What's wrong with that?"

"Nothing is wrong with enjoying friends. But I'm concerned that you take advantage of the things that are out there. Music, art, sports. I don't care what you choose, but it's important that you really give something a shot. You'll feel good at having stuck with something. It can't feel okay walking away every time something seems like a drag. And once you get through the rough spots you may really enjoy yourself."

"But I don't feel like anything . . ." she insists stubbornly.

"That may be, but that's not acceptable. I'm not saying you have to stick with something forever, either. Choose something and let's agree on a time. Say, six months."

"Okay, okay . . ." she mutters. "What do you want me to do?"

"Uh-uh." You shake your head vigorously. "What you do is your choice. This is something I want for you. Not for me."

"I'll do the flute . . ." She sighs. "It's just that this piece is hard to play . . ."

"Do the best you can," you comment. "That's all I care about."

"Okay," she says, slightly annoyed.

Don't expect any better than that now. She hasn't felt the pleasures of an accomplishment yet. Enthusiasm will come when she allows herself the progress she's been denying herself to date.

Your Twelve-Year-Old

Your twelve-year-old daughter has had it with Sunday school. She's got other things on her mind these days, and doesn't like the additional pressure. She's been obstreperous about many things lately, and you've tried to bend on most. But this issue is one upon which you intend to stand your ground.

It's late September, she's attended twice, grumbling all the way, and now it's the third Sunday, and she has come downstairs with little time to spare, still in her nightgown.

"Honey," you say evenly, "you better get dressed. We're due to leave in ten minutes."

"I'm not going," Jessica replies. "I'm tired of it."

"I know you have lots of other work and things you want to do, but I'm sure you can squeeze it in later. Sunday school is only two hours."

"No. I'm not going," Jessica repeats, reaching into the refrigerator for some orange juice.

"Is there some special problem you're having there you haven't told me about?"

"No," Jessica answers.

"Then go get dressed," you say flatly. "You're going. Sunday school is very important to this family. It's meaningful and explores issues about our heritage and our inner selves, which I want you to think about. And that's it.''

Jessica is now standing there, stubbornly glaring at you. ''You can't boss me around.''

''I try not to.'' You nod. ''I don't like that feeling, either. But I'm your parent and every once in a while I have to put my foot down about something I feel is extremely important.''

''I DON'T WANT TO GO,'' Jessica insists.

''Go upstairs now,'' you say sharply. ''If you continue to talk to me this way, you will lose your telephone privileges for a week. You are going to Sunday school no matter what you do or say, but if you make it intolerable for me, that's the price you'll pay.''

''Fine,'' she snaps as she turns to go upstairs.

She will likely come downstairs sullen, but dressed.

If she does not, clearly you won't be able to carry her out to the car. But you can certainly consider changing the no-phone week to as long as it takes for her to return to Sunday school. Plus one week.

Sooner or later she'll go.

TECHNIQUE #11

THE BETTER WAY TO BRIBE

WORKS FOR: GETTING YOUR CHILD TO BEHAVE RESPONSIBLY—
CHANGE A BAD HABIT—DO AS YOU ASK SUCH AS CLEAN HIS
ROOM, LEAVE A PARTY, KEEP HIS HAT ON—TRY NEW THINGS—
TOLERATE UNPLEASANT EXPERIENCES SUCH AS A
VISIT TO THE DENTIST.

THE TECHNIQUE

First, understand that the word bribe covers a lot of territory. And it's not all bad.

Anytime one person gives another person a "reward" for doing something they would not have done otherwise, it can be termed a bribe. Which means, when you think about it, that a great portion of the workforce in this country is technically being bribed!

There is, then, a subcategory of bribe that comes under the heading of Positive Incentive. That's how the workforce functions, and that's what you want to aim for as a parent.

Here's how to tell the difference. If you are offering a reward on the spot out of desperation, then, you are, strictly speaking, offering a bribe. A child who won't leave a party, and is told, "Look, come now and when we get home I'll play Chutes and Ladders with you," is being bribed. Though it sounds as if you're the one speaking it's your child who is saying, "I'm not going

to do what you want. So what'cha gonna do about it?''
A child who is told before the party, ''You often have
trouble leaving parties. If you behave yourself when I
tell you it's time to go, we'll play whatever game you
want when we get home,'' is being properly motivated.
Here you're saying, ''This is how I'd like you to behave
and this is what will happen if you do. It's your choice.''

Big difference.

Specifically here's how it works. Basically set up your
reward in advance. Continue to do this for like circumstances (leaving a play date, coming home directly after
school instead of dawdling), varying the reward. It may
on occasion be material. A small gift can be at times
appropriate. But so is a favorite meal, special time with
you, an extra play date, a brief outing, and for older kids,
more time on the phone. After a while you will be able
to move from more concrete rewards to ones of a more
subtle nature. For instance, for younger children lots of
praise and a new ''big boy'' privilege, and for older,
allowing your child to finish his homework at a time of
his choosing. By the time you drop the promise of a
reward, your child will have moved from being totally
motivated externally to an internal motivation as well.
He will enjoy the pleasure of, for instance, not ruining
the aftermath of a fun party by getting into a fight. He
will enjoy your approval and the sense of camaraderie
between the two of you. And he will gain a strong sense
of self in being able to control his own impulses and
earn your trust.

Of course, if you've gotten into a bad pattern of brib-
ing on the spot it's going to be tough to break it. But
it's only a matter of time before your child gets the message. Each time he says, ''Well, if I do that can I have

a cookie, or can we go to the toy store?'' you will simply say, ''No. No more of that. But I'll tell you what. I'll give you a penny each time you go food shopping and you don't make it difficult. After you've collected five pennies, then we can go across the street and get you those stickers you like.''

That's not a bribe. He doesn't have you in a spot. Neither one of you is really cornered. Rather, you're on a bicycle built for two and if he wants to get someplace it's up to him to follow the trail you've laid out. (Do note that it wouldn't be fair to suddenly start giving negative consequences for poor behavior, in place of the usual bribe. After all, you helped create the problem.)

WHY IT WORKS:

First, let's take a look at why ineffective bribery doesn't work.

Offering a reward, on the spot, to put an end to unacceptable behavior does nothing for helping a child develop an inner motivation or find value in less obvious rewards. He becomes addicted to needing something each time he performs, and you become trapped in the tango.

Your child gains an unrealistic view of the world, and you will become resentful over his demandingness, lack of generosity, seeming selfishness, and manipulativeness.

But presenting a child with a positive incentive should he choose to behave in a way that he knows you would like, gives him power over himself, not you. The more he is able to control his impulses, and gain a reward, the more time he will experience the other side benefits—the ones that will lead him to cooperate later, concrete reward or not. He will start to feel more independent, adult, and more in sync with you.

After you have been consistent for a while with a concrete reward, and you sense he is enjoying the understanding between you, and as you begin to change the reward to something much less concrete, he will be able to see the benefits of meeting your expectations. "You know, I'm tired this evening and so I don't think I can play Monopoly, but you've been so agreeable lately, I think I'm going to start letting you stay up a half hour later at night to play with your puzzle books." The next time you ask him to leave a friend's house, or clean up his room, he will not wait for a reward. The focus of the behavior will not entirely be on the anticipation of what is to come. Other rewards in the form of privileges will have taken on new meaning. He will have a chance to discover that in the end, a hug accompanied by a "You're a very good kid," will give him a far warmer feeling than a new superhero figure.

And that being a "good kid" means he's going to be the recipient of your goodwill. He will begin to do what you expect because, in general, after having done it he feels good.

Proud even.

THE DEEPER MESSAGE

Actually, it's more an issue of the "deeper lesson."

While it is true the world works well when good behaviors reap rewards, it is also true that it would fall apart if each and every time, one was expected. It would fly in the face of reality. Sometimes rewards cannot be forthcoming. Sometimes a person has to enjoy his own success or selflessness simply for its own sake. Sometimes a person has to offer a reward instead of receiving one and in so doing, find the pleasure in that.

By saying to your child "thank you for helping me," instead of handing him a dollar, you're reminding him that someone other than he has needs. And that cooperating or pitching in is an end in itself.

Your child has to learn to see himself in context.

Only when he's very young does the Lone Ranger fantasy have any value!

SEEING IT IN ACTION:

Your Four-Year-Old

You have been visiting friends and now it's time to go.

The only thing is, as usual, Timmy cannot be budged from the electric train set. He is hypnotized by the flashing lights and the intricately woven track over which a bright red train is wending its way.

You've been through this before with him and this morning you'd been very clear. "Timmy, if you leave nicely this evening when we get home I will read you three whole books before you go to sleep."

"Okay," he'd said brightly.

But apparently he's forgotten.

You've already given him an extra five minutes, but he's intractable.

"NOOO!!!" he screams as you try to slip his winter parka on. "NO!!! ONE MORE TIME!!!"

You've had it and you can tell your hosts are anxious to clean up and get ready for bed. You are unbelievably tempted to whisper in his ear, "Timmy, if you come right now I'll let you have that last cupcake in the box at home."

You feel embarrassed at the thought, looking around furtively to see if anyone would hear if you gave into this temptation. No one would, but something stops you. Timmy can't be allowed to rule the roost.

Instead, you bend down and firmly say, "Timmy, we made a deal this evening. You either leave now nicely, or we'll carry you out and you'll go straight to bed with no books."

Chances are he'll go.

(Clearly you needn't be too rigid about the deal you made. Your younger child may need a reminder. Just because he's starting to behave poorly is not a strong reason to back out of the deal. If once you remind him he chooses to ignore you, *then* you can show him you meant business.)

But what if you hadn't issued an earlier warning? What if this was surprise behavior? Could you just offer him the cupcake anyway?

You could, but you'll be setting up a dangerous precedent. It's far better to name a consequence in this instance than to offer a bribe. "If you don't come nicely now, there will be no dessert tomorrow," will do just as well as, "If you come now, I'll give you some candy when we get home."

If you haven't been cookie and candying him to death in the past you will absolutely get away with it. If you have, you'll just have to weather the storm, pick him up, and bring him home. A few more episodes like this and he'll get it.

Your Eight-Year-Old

Allan hates trying anything new. He's a perfectionist and unless he's quite sure he will excel, he doesn't want to give new pursuits a try.

You would very much like to take him ice-skating. You're sure that once he gets the hang of it he'll enjoy it very much.

The trouble is he doesn't want to go.

He didn't want to go last Saturday when you suggested it. Or the Saturday before that.

You've refrained from a bribe because you've felt it would be good for him to voluntarily arrive at the point where trying something new doesn't have to be such a big deal.

But this is clearly a dream.

And so, somewhat reluctantly, you say, "I'll tell you what. Go with me. If you give it a real try, afterward I'll take you to that movie you've been wanting to see."

You feel slimy, though, because it seems like you're not helping him at all and are being very manipulated.

Nothing could be further from the truth.

A very reluctant child often needs an incentive to get over his own hesitation. Rather than being manipulative you are being downright helpful.

He may not see it that way, he may dejectedly say, "Okay" as if he's been trapped. But ignore it. You feel ice-skating is a fun thing to try. And you know if he hates it you will let him stop in short order.

You've fixed things so he can't hurt himself by saying "no." You've given him something to keep his mind on, while he struggles to overcome his anxieties.

Your Twelve-Year-Old

Julia doesn't listen very well. She's a bit of an early bloomer. Already the boys are giving her the eye and you're worried you are going to have trouble keeping her to curfew, getting her off the phone, and helping her see a cute guy isn't everything.

In short, it's going to be hard to slow her down.

She's asked to go out with some friends Friday evening to the neighborhood pizza shop and you want her home no later than eight. You don't want to fight about it and you certainly don't want her to make it difficult for both of you by not adhering to the rule.

And so you lay the future out on the line. It's a constructive bribe. But it's also a kind of warning. Only instead of saying what bad things will happen if she doesn't arrive home at eight, you speak of the good things that will come of her prompt appearance.

"Julia, I'm going to let you go. But I want you home by eight. I think I can trust you to do that. If it turns out I'm right, I'll be much more relaxed about letting you go out other times as well. I do want you to have fun. So watch the clock. Otherwise, it will be hard for me to say 'yes' next time."

Say it with a smile. The carrot is your trust and her deserved freedom. In the bargain you will be getting a happy child who does what you ask because she knows you'll deal fairly with her. And in the process she will develop a real sense of pride in her growing independence.

TECHNIQUE #12

SHOCK VALUE

WORKS FOR: STOPPING POOR BEHAVIOR ON THE SPOT—
DRAWING ATTENTION TO SPECIFIC GOOD BEHAVIOR—
ILLUSTRATING A POINT WORDS CANNOT EXPRESS.

THE TECHNIQUE

Take an unexpected, dramatic action to effect a change in your child's behavior. Don't reprimand. Don't increase a consequence. Don't negotiate. Do something startling that will not only stop your child in his tracks but make him realize you really mean what you've been saying.

If your children won't stop arguing over dinner, take your plate upstairs and eat in bed! If your son behaved well at a family get-together, write him a note thanking him and put it in the mail. If your daughter won't stop telling little lies, tell one of your own and let her see what it feels like.

Do not, however, overuse the technique. Pick and choose your moments. Otherwise, the unexpected will become expected and completely lose its impact.

WHY IT WORKS

A shock tends to focus attention.

Your unexpected action will immediately make an impression. Your child will be forced to think about what he did or has been doing simply to make sense of your behavior!

You haven't just told him it's time to sit up and listen. You've shown him.

It should be noted that this technique will work a little better with older children as they are more sensitive to unusual behavior patterns than a younger child might be. However, using shock to stop a sibling squabble, such as abruptly leaving the room saying, "Bye now! Have fun!" for instance, can work well, as the younger child will not only witness your behavior but will also take his cue from the older sibling's surprise.

When you do something for shock value, you draw vigorous attention to an issue. Your child may feel hurt, amused, appreciated, incredulous, betrayed, or angry. But one thing is for sure.

He will pay attention.

THE DEEPER MESSAGE

There is no room for discussion. You will not be drawn into a debate or argument. You have determined it's time to inform, unequivocally.

You are willing to go to great and unusual lengths to demonstrate what you mean.

SEEING IT IN ACTION:

Your Four-Year-Old

Ethan and his eight-year-old brother have been battling in the back seat of the car since you took off for your beach vacation two hours ago.

You gave them coloring and activity books but they did no good. You tried to both joke them out of their annoyance with each other, as well as distract them with travel games.

But nothing worked.

Finally, you and your wife raised your voices a few times, threatening to go home, or stop the car, or skip lunch. But to no avail.

And so you make your move.

Checking carefully for traffic flow, you pull over to the side of the busy highway as far off the thoroughfare as possible. You turn around calmly and say to your children, "We don't want to listen to your arguing anymore. It's too hard to drive. We're going to get out of the car and stand in the sun a while. You stay here and sort out your differences. We'll continue when you're through."

And then do just that. Open the door and stand at the side of the road a few yards away from the car. Chat amicably. No angry gesturing. No loud words. Make it clear, it's simply that you've had enough. You're not leaving them. You just don't want to be around them.

Your four-year-old will get a sense for the incongruity

of the situation as he watches his older brother stare after you in astonishment.

After a reasonable period of time, approximately five full minutes, return to the car.

It will likely be very quiet, though one or both children might meekly say, "How come you did that?"

"Because you weren't listening and we simply couldn't stand the noise," you reply quietly.

And that, will likely, be that.

Your Nine-Year-Old

You've been having a difficult time with your son Peter. He's been very argumentative and uncooperative lately and you've gotten into a pattern of very unpleasant arguments. You think it might have something to do with his father's new job, which has him traveling out of town quite a bit. But even so, Peter's behavior has become unacceptable.

The other evening, however, was different. You had an old friend over for dinner with her five-year-old son. You had worried that Peter would take one look at him and walk off to sullenly read a book. Before they arrived you gently asked him to spend a little time with the child, and Peter had merely shrugged. A bad sign, you had thought.

But you were wrong.

Instead, Peter took the little boy under his wing and very good-naturedly led him on an evening-long tour of his room, clearly basking in the younger boy's admiration of him and his belongings.

That evening after tucking Peter into bed and complimenting him on his behavior, you wrote him a note, enclosed an IOU for an afternoon movie and mailed it the next morning.

When it arrived you left the envelope on Peter's bed.

Now Peter walks in the door and grumpily asks for a snack. You give it to him and listen as he walks upstairs to do his homework.

A few minutes later you hear him on his way down again. He walks into the living room with a funny look on his face.

"What'ja do that for?" he asks, looking pleased but a little off balance.

"Because you were such a great host the other night," you say matter-of-factly. "I was so proud and I wanted you to know that. It was important to me that you treated Joey well."

Peter nods, staring down at the IOU.

"So what movie?" you ask good-naturedly.

"Not sure yet," Peter answers thoughtfully.

"Fine, just let me know. In the meantime, honey, go finish your homework." You tense, waiting for something approaching a snarl.

"Okay," Peter agrees and takes the steps two at a time back up to his room, clearly forgetting to put on the usual sneer.

Your Twelve-Year-Old

Jillian has begun telling little lies.

She claims she's brushed her teeth, when she hasn't. That her homework is done, when it isn't. That she didn't hit her little sister, when she did.

It's gotten to the point where you are not at all clear you can believe anything she claims is true. Given that she is entering that scary time of adolescence where she is going to be seeking increased independence, this state of affairs is making you very anxious. You need to set her straight now.

You've tried explaining why lying is so unacceptable—that it's disrespectful, that it inspires distrust, and that it makes the listener feel belittled and cheated. You've even explained how it can get a person into serious trouble, something Jillian has already experienced. (She told a lie to a friend only to be found out shortly thereafter with the end result being she almost lost two friends.)

But nothing seems to work.

And so you decide to make a more dramatic point.

"Can we go shopping tomorrow morning?" Jillian asks Friday evening. "I need new sneakers and a sweater to wear to Annie's party."

"That would be fine," you say nodding agreeably.

The next morning, Jillian flies downstairs at nine-thirty all dressed and ready to go. "Ready to go shopping?" she asks as she pours herself a glass of orange juice.

"Actually I can't go," you say evenly as you continue to leaf through the paper.

"Wh . . . what do you mean you can't go . . . ?" Jillian practically sputters as she stares at you wide-eyed. "You said you could go."

"I did, but it wasn't true. I just didn't want you to harass me about it so I said yes," you explain.

"BUT THAT'S NOT FAIR!" Jillian cries out.

"No, it isn't," you answer calmly. "Nor is it fair when you claim to have finished your homework, or cleaned up your room, or helped your sister, when you didn't.''

Jillian is struck dumb at this.

You remain quiet, letting your point sink in.

Finally, Jillian looking a little beaten down, sighs. "Yeah. Okay. I get the point. But I still need new sneakers and a new sweater.''

"The party is next week," you inform her. "We'll go another day. In the meantime, did you clean up your room?"

"Yes, I . . ." Jillian stops herself cold.

"Clean it up, please." You smile at her. "Bad habits are hard to break, aren't they?!''

You can use a little humor. You made your point dramatically enough. This doesn't have to be a Greek tragedy.

See It His Way: Be Realistic!

WORKS FOR: *GENERATING A SENSE WITHIN YOUR CHILD THAT YOU UNDERSTAND HIS WORLD AND HE CAN TRUST YOU TO ACT IN ACCORDANCE WITH WHAT YOU KNOW.*

THE TECHNIQUE

Whether it's recognizing what the "other kids" wear, or understanding that nine o'clock might be too early a curfew for your twelve-year-old's party, or levying a consequence, take the time to accurately perceive the world within which your child travels. If you think his homework notebook is too gimmicky, take a look at his friend's. Even though you might choose to serve health cookies, consider the possible emotional damage of not allowing your child to eat a regular cookie at a friend's house. If you are going to issue a consequence, consider what you can make stick and what you can't.

Naturally, if everyone is being allowed to do something of which you don't approve, you have to put your foot down. But it is unlikely that an entire group of kids is being given inappropriate permission for anything. So take a good long look at what your child is up against, and increase the possibility of one, her "fitting in," and two, her listening to and respecting your rules.

WHY IT WORKS

Children want to live on the same planet as their parents. It leaves them feeling "known." There is an old saying by Ralph Waldo Emerson that goes "It is a luxury to be understood" and indeed it is. The need to feel the same, "to be cool," can affect a child as young as four.

Children don't like to feel different. This becomes especially acute during adolescence.

As a parent you will want to convey your understanding of this need, because not to do so would fail to generate a key component of a healthy relationship with your child.

Trusting communication.

Children are on a never-ending ambivalent quest to separate from parents. They want to grow up but they want to stay little. They want to strike out on their own, but they want to know they can come home and be protected. A parent who consistently fails to understand a child's world will be easily written off. "She just doesn't get it," the child will think. It will feed into her impulse to pay the parent little attention, and in so doing she will miss out on a critical protection, guidance, and support. The parent, in effect, will be giving the child permission to separate long before she can safely do so.

But a parent will also be ruining *trust*. Your child needs to know she can count on you. That the words you offer are indeed the *help* you profess them to be. It is critical to keep the lines of communication open. Your child needs to feel that he can ask for permission to do things and that you will understand and when possible say yes. She needs this in order to obey the "nos." She also needs to see that she can tell you how she feels and not have you visit an expectation upon her that is out of sync with her abilities or age.

In order to keep your child wanting your advice and guidance and ready to share the problems in her life, you will want to be as realistic as possible about the issues with which she is dealing. Sure, if a classmate cheats off her paper she should tell the teacher. But is that wise for her socially? Yes, you may only permit organic and health cookies, but is it fair to expect your eight-year-old to turn down a chocolate layer cake at a friend's house? And, of course, you may think the aqua-blue flannel shirt is great, but if all the kids wear plaid must you insist he wear it or there's no dessert?

The same is true for unrealistic consequences. When you do it right you're letting your child know that you know what will work. He may hate your dead-on accuracy, but deep inside he'll be glad he's not the one in control.

When you can understand what your child's concerns are from his world perspective, and use this information to tailor your support and guidance you will be bringing up a child who knows the deeper message.

THE DEEPER MESSAGE

Knowing your child's world, even though it clearly differs from what you might like, says to your child, "I love you no matter what and I want to understand the way things are for you."

You are creating an atmosphere in which he can tell you about the temptations he experiences without fear of your judgment or a negative repercussion. The message is that it's more important for you to hear him out, to see all aspects of an issue and to talk, than it is for you to jump in and exercise your authority.

Also, you are minimizing his guilt, an emotion that inevitably leads to anger. While your child might sneak around your back if he believes you are being unreasonable, he won't feel good about it. For one thing, it's frightening and for another, it will make him feel "bad." This in turn can evolve into rage and then more undesirable behavior.

And finally, when you are realistic in your demands you are modeling flexibility (see technique #13)—a key skill in moving through life. You are showing your child that there is much about life one can't plan in advance. And that certain rules or ideals can't always be adhered to under certain circumstances. One needs to see the whole picture, look at the pluses and minuses, and then make appropriate decisions. When a child learns to be flexible within the family, he takes this out into the world and will find it eminently useful in his work and social growth. And most importantly it will help him make the decisions he needs to make free of guilt.

He can adapt free of excess "baggage."

SEEING IT IN ACTION:

Your Four-Year-Old

Lisa has a sweet tooth. Actually, you realize, most children do, but you cannot abide the amount and kind of candy you see them eating. You determined long ago that there would be none of that "sweet stuff" in your home.

But Lisa and Mindy have just gotten back to your house from a friend's birthday party. Gleefully, they spill the contents of their goody bags onto the floor. Out falls a little rubber ball, pretend lipstick, a tiny bag of M&M's, and a lollipop. Seconds later Mindy has ripped off the paper and is noisily sucking on the pop, but Lisa you notice is staring at hers tensely, slowly but surely edging the pop off the table. You're not sure if she intends to ease the paper off or hide it.

But you can see the indecision and confusion etched across her face.

And you can also see the monumental pleasure Mindy is clearly experiencing as she bounces the ball about the room licking away at the candy. Lisa hasn't missed it, either.

One candy once in a while, you tell yourself sternly, won't matter. Be flexible (see technique #3). You can't expect Lisa to resist the candy with Mindy right there.

"Lisa, it's okay," you say humorously. "How can you not when Mindy is enjoying hers so much right in front of you! Go ahead. This is an exception."

By telling her exactly what your reasoning is you are letting her know you are seeing what she sees. You are understanding her. And importantly to you, it has nothing to do with your rules about candy. They still apply. But, Mindy, the party, and the lollipop constitute a good reason to do things a bit differently this once.

And you are relieving your daughter of guilt. "How can you not want . . . ?" is another way of saying, "How you feel is totally reasonable to me!"

Your Nine-Year-Old

You were brought up by very formal parents and were taught early to shake people's hands when you greet them.

This is something you have passed along to your son. As a seven-year-old he gamely shook everyone's hand too. But now, a self-conscious fourth grader, he's refusing to greet anyone in this fashion. "Nobody does that," he snaps at you unhappily. "Don't make me." The last time you brought him anywhere, the moment of truth was so loaded that not only did he not extend his hand, he could hardly bring himself to look the person in the eye.

You are, of course, tempted to say you don't much care what anyone does. Shaking hands is the polite thing to do. But it occurs to you that there might be something to what your son is saying. And so at a neighbor's holiday party you look around. In truth, no child under sixteen shakes hands with any adult.

It's not right, you think, but your son's observation is correct. It's understandable, then, why shaking someone's hand would embarrass him. The question becomes, you realize, how can you teach your son to politely greet someone without the handshake?

How can you satisfy both of your needs?

On the way home from the party you turn to your son. "Listen, Josh, I noticed you were right. Kids your age aren't shaking hands much. But it's important to be polite, so here's what I suggest. I won't expect you to shake someone's hand, unless, of course, they extend their own hand. But I do expect you to look them in the eye, say hello, and smile. Deal?"

Your son will more than likely nod enthusiastically.

But not just because he doesn't have to shake hands.

He'll be happy his parent "gets it."

Your Twelve-Year-Old

Jessica has, for the fifth time in three weeks, left a book at school that is necessary to complete her homework.

You are absolutely furious and inform her that you have had it. She cannot hang out after school for any reason at all with the other kids for one whole month. And then angrily you step out of her room, struck, you realize, by one thing.

Jessica doesn't look all that upset.

Seconds later you know why.

You really can't enforce this. Sometimes she needs to go to the library after school, other times there's an after-school extracurricular meeting. She can squeeze social time in whenever she feels like it.

You think about this for an hour and then return to Jessica's room where she is now working on a book report. "I've been thinking about what I said about a whole month of coming straight home. It's not going to work. I can't know what you're doing after school all the time and I'm afraid you'd get tempted to just hang out and I wouldn't blame you. Besides, I can't insist you be here ten minutes after the bell rings because you have other responsibilities."

Your daughter will probably look up with great surprise.

"So, since you forgot your math book at school and

I estimate it would take about forty-five minutes to complete an evening's assignment, I think you should do a job around the house that will take the same amount of time. Please collect all the laundry in the house and bring it down to the basement and then report to me in the den for further instructions.''

Then walk out.

This will absolutely horrify your twelve-year-old, but it is a nicely wrought fair trade and she will know it. It's also one that you can supervise and it's very realistic. Demanding that she come home could give temptation a chance to win, but also inconvenience others (such as if she's in a band). She knows that won't work and will fully expect that as the days go by you will simply ''forget'' about the month edict.

But now Jessica knows you've got a plan. A real plan. One that she can't play with and which is quite workable. Just hateful.

She trudges downstairs to do the wash, a little surprised at the corner she's gotten herself into . . . and begrudgingly respectful of just how you managed to help her there.

Tomorrow she'll remember her homework. Otherwise, you might have her mopping the floors.

LIES EQUAL DOUBLE TROUBLE

WORKS FOR: GETTING A CHILD TO STOP LYING IN THE MIDST OF DOING SO—NOT TO LIE IN THE FUTURE—UNDERSTAND THE IMPORTANCE OF TRUTH.

THE TECHNIQUE

All children lie. When they're younger they do it out of a confused sense of right and wrong. Many times it's wishful thinking. ("Not me! I didn't break that bowl!") As children get older they do it to keep out of trouble. But it is critical for them to realize that in your family, and indeed in the outside world, lying more often than not gets people into worse trouble.

You will want to make it clear, with complete consistency that lying is unacceptable. One simple way to do this, after one warning, is double the consequences. Two days of no TV becomes four. But not in a vacuum, and not with preschoolers:

- If you catch your child in a lie ask him why he felt the need to cover the truth. You need to know if he was afraid of your anger, loss of love, or simply the punishment.
- Be careful not to make any punishment so hei-

nous that your child would do *anything* to avoid it. This will only encourage lies.

- If he insists he didn't lie in the face of all sorts of evidence that he did, calmly ask him why he is doing this. In other words, take the emphasis away from an outright admission, and turn it into a discussion about why he would deny something so rigorously when the facts are clear. Try not to allow your anger to skyrocket along with his insistence. It will only make it that much harder for him to face the truth.

- If he continues to lie about many things, or persists in one lie in particular beyond the point of reason, try asking the question, "What do you think will happen to you if the truth comes out?"

- When your child opts not to lie and tell you the truth, be sure to praise him and *still* offer a consequence. "I'm so glad you told me. I feel that I can trust you. No after-school biking tomorrow, but if you'd lied it would have been two days."

- Whatever you do, though it can be difficult, try not to view your child's lie as a betrayal. It can feel extraordinarily painful to listen to your child tell a story that is blatantly untrue. It can almost feel as if he's mocking you.

  But he isn't. He's just protecting himself. He needs to learn, of course, that there are better ways than lying to do this, and that telling an untruth can be quite painful and insulting. This can be helped along through "How would you feel if I . . ." conversations.

- Also, try and honestly assess if you are a parent to whom it's hard to bring bad news? Do you react with powerful, frightening emotions? If so, you're setting the stage for lies.

A lie is not a tragedy. But it is the act of a child who is hiding something. Either he's afraid of what he's done or he's afraid of you. In either case, you can help matters considerably if your child knows that you will keep a wrongdoing in perspective and his needs met. (See techniques #6 and #8).

WHY IT WORKS

Lying is not a pleasant experience. No matter what side of the fence you are on, it makes for very uncomfortable feelings.

In short, given an option your child would probably rather not lie. It's just that he doesn't want to get into trouble or lose a privilege or not do what he wants to do.

Getting at the bottom of what he was hoping for by lying, and doubling the punishment will clarify his expectations and yours. If it's fear of your anger you will need to explain that a lot of it is disappointment and hurt. That you had thought there was the kind of trust between you, which allows for making mistakes. You want him to tell you if he's done something wrong and while he may receive a consequence, you'll be a lot less upset than if he doubles the wrong by lying about it.

And, of course, if it's simply a matter of him wanting to do what he wants and knowing if he asks you'll say no, then after he receives a consequence for lying, you might want to discuss each of your positions. Maybe you're being too strict. Maybe he's trying to behave older than his years. Maybe there's room for compromise. But even if there is, you're making it clear that the lie is the biggest problem of all.

For the most part kids do get caught in lies. They know this. Sooner or later you'll find out he went to a friend's house instead of the library, she did take her sister's favorite doll, and that he changed the grade on his book report.

By making it clear that the lie will double the punishment he will think twice about taking the chance, knowing that the odds of the simple mistake coming to light are overwhelming anyway.

THE DEEPER MESSAGE

The clear message that lying is completely unacceptable in your family will sensitize your child enough to the issue that he is unlikely to do it easily outside of the family. Lying, he will realize, can bring serious consequences.

Raising an inherently honest child who does not feel belittled by facing his own mistakes but rather courageous for doing so, is an important goal. By praising him for owning up to a mistake, you are placing his honesty above his weakness. This fact will not be lost on your child even in light of a consequence.

And he will feel appreciated and loved for exactly who he is, flaws and all.

SEEING IT IN ACTION:

Your Four-Year-Old

It's three days after Halloween. You've taken Will's candy and put it in the kitchen cupboard, explaining that you will allow him one piece every day.

Earlier that afternoon you'd given him a piece of chocolate, washed his face, and then sent him into the playroom with his buddy. But now it's right before dinner. You happen to glance down and see the telltale marks of another piece of chocolate smudged all over his lips.

"Will, you took another piece of chocolate?" you say, more as a statement than a question.

"NO," he replies stubbornly. "I didn't!"

You are tempted to ask him if he's sure, but that would end up inviting him to lie again.

"Well, I'll tell you what," you say matter-of-factly, "let me show you why I think you did."

Gently lead him over to a mirror and point out the chocolate smudge. "See that?" you ask. "That's what gave it away!"

Caught, Will just stands there looking a little nervous.

"I didn't mean to . . . it was the one piece you said I could have . . . I forgot I had a piece . . ."

You nod. "I know. It was so tempting. All that chocolate up there. But you know, honey, I told you only one piece. And I meant one piece. You have to remember that."

You don't accuse him of lying. He's not sure what he

was doing and to accuse him of that would hurt terribly. Instead, you demonstrate that it's hard to get away with a lie. That saying something that isn't true (or wishing something that is true isn't) is no answer.

This is an important step toward your four-year-old's development of a conscience.

Your Nine-Year-Old

It's almost time for Alex to come home from school, when you get a call from the principal, informing you that two days ago he hit someone during recess and was supposed to bring a note home for you to sign. But twice now, he's come to school without it.

You, of course, have never heard of this note, and so you thank the principal very much and tell him you'll take care of it. You know Alex has a hot temper. This hitting issue has been a problem before.

Just then your son walks in, and, of course, you're steaming.

"Hi, Mom!" he calls out like an angel.

"Hello," you say, keeping your anger in check. You remind yourself that kids do this kind of thing a lot. "Do you have anything for me today from school?" you ask, giving him one last chance.

"No," he says calmly, rummaging about in the cookie jar.

"Well, I just got a phone call from the principal," you promptly inform him. There's no point setting him up with such statements as "ARE YOU SURE?" You're just elongating his lie and ultimately frustrating yourself.

"He says you have a note. In fact, you've had a note

for a few days that says you misbehaved during recess and I'm supposed to sign it.''

''Oh,'' Alex says, looking down at the floor. ''Well, I lost it.''

''I see.'' You nod. ''So why didn't you tell me about it at least?''

Alex shrugs. ''I forgot.''

''I doubt that,'' you say matter-of-factly. ''You were probably just hoping I wouldn't find out.''

He shrugs again.

''You know, Alex, I'm not happy about you getting into trouble at recess, and I'd like to hear exactly what you did, but what's making me very upset is that you lied.''

''I DID NOT!'' Alex protests. ''I didn't say anything!''

''That's a lie,'' you explain. ''Not bringing home the letter was, in effect, saying, 'I didn't get a letter.' But you did get a letter.''

''I'm sorry,'' Alex says meekly.

''Well, I would have taken away TV privileges for two days for the hitting. You know your father and I have talked to you a lot about using words instead of your hands when you get angry. But because of the fact that you didn't bring home the letter, the TV is off limits for four whole days.''

''THAT'S NOT FAIR,'' Alex cries out.

''It is fair. You lied. You know that is unacceptable in this house. Besides, honey, what did you think would happen? Surely you knew we'd find out about the letter? What did you think I was going to do?''

''I don't know . . .'' Alex mutters. ''I knew you'd get mad.''

"So what?" you say evenly. "So what if I'm mad? I still love you." Then you smile. "Even though you don't get TV for four nights. Period. Lying gets twice the consequence. And you know it."

Alex shuffles away, probably extremely relieved. Somewhere inside he knew you'd find out. The consequence is unpleasant, but it's not horrible. Next time, he tells himself, he'll own up his mistake. That way he doesn't have to miss a week of *The Simpsons*.

Your Twelve-Year-Old

You have a feeling your son did not go to the library after school, but, in fact, went out with a group of friends. You think this because he did not come home with any library books, but instead claimed to have forgotten them there after taking notes.

"Are you telling me the truth?" you ask quietly.

"Yes," he insists.

"Can I see your notes?" you ask.

"I accidentally left those in the library, too . . ." he says firmly.

You're in a spot. Every fiber of your being says he didn't go. But you cannot accuse him when you have no proof. Instead, you opt for something of a mini-moral lecture.

"I hope that's true. I wouldn't be happy if you missed the library today, but I'd be especially disappointed if you lied about it. That's the thing that would upset me most. You needed to go to the library today, because you had important work to get done and it would be avoiding your responsibility if you didn't. But lying to me about it would be even worse."

You see your son hesitate. He's a good kid. You can tell he's growing very uneasy inside.

But he doesn't say a word.

There's nothing more you can do.

He's going to have to wrestle with his conscience.

It's going to feel extremely uncomfortable.

Chances are he won't do this again. At least not for a while!

Don't Make a Mistake a Sin or Kids Are Supposed to Mess Up

WORKS FOR: HANDLING ANY MISSTEP YOUR CHILD MIGHT MAKE BIG OR SMALL, IN A MANNER THAT ADDRESSES THE INFRACTION, BUT RETAINS HIS SELF-ESTEEM.

THE TECHNIQUE

First, no matter what the misbehavior, remind yourself that there is far more to your child than his capacity to err. Besides, making mistakes is human. He's still learning right from wrong, developing a social conscience and figuring out how to deal with temptation. Slipping up, no matter how dramatically, is often part of the process.

Second, when your first reaction is that your child has committed a seemingly unforgivable act, take another look. Is it so bad? Could you understand how it might have happened? Can you see, why, from her perspective it isn't so bad?

Third, the next time your child does something wrong, stay specific. Don't generalize. And don't blow the problem out of proportion, even if it's big.

When your child forgets for the fifth time to write down his homework assignment, don't yell, "You are so irresponsible! I cannot count on you to remember anything!'' but rather say, ''This homework thing has got to stop. You must start taking your assignments seriously. You have to take responsibility for your work.''

If your child does something more serious, such as admit to shoplifting an item, don't turn him into a criminal with no hope of redemption. ''I didn't know you were so dishonest. How could you? Aren't you ashamed?'' should be replaced by, ''Stealing is wrong. I know you know that. Why did you do it?''

Time is much better spent trying to get to the root of any misbehavior than it is prophesying doom. And it is critical that you convey a sort of ''relativity'' about life. This is bad. This is a little better. This isn't great, but . . . The ability to see things in perspective is a valuable tool for successfully moving through the ups and downs of life.

WHY IT WORKS

It is damaging to anyone to feel as if a mistake can simply wipe them off the map. Erase all the good. It is such a painful feeling, in fact, that little time can be spent on understanding and facing the misstep. Every bit of energy is needed to hang on to one's sense of self and reality.

But it is not damaging to be reprimanded and receive consequences for a specific behavior. The focus stays clear. The whole being is not called into question. Your child can think about what's happened, well aware that he has neither lost you nor himself.

Also, depending on the sort of child you're dealing with, if you treat every mistake as if the world is going to end, and he's not the type to shrink away, he could easily stop taking your anger seriously. He won't think, "Wow. She's really mad. I didn't realize what I was doing is that bad." Rather, he'll shrug to himself and think, "There she goes again. I wonder what's on TV tonight."

THE DEEPER MESSAGE

It is very important for everyone to be forgiving of themselves. We cannot be perfect, and to expect it of ourselves is to leave us feeling woefully inadequate. Your child needs to understand that while he should strive to do his best, along the way he will stumble. He should expect to pay the price.

But a reasonable price.

And then he should move on, free of the notion that somehow he is now, less than.

This is a healthy and constructive attitude that will also spill over into the way he deals with others. A forgiving person who can accept other's weaknesses will function very positively in social relationships.

But perhaps most importantly, by regulating your response to your child's mistakes, by remaining specific and not getting as angry over a lost glove as you would an out-and-out lie, you are teaching your child about life and the art of emotional discrimination. Not every problem or mistake is as big or small as another, nor does it require the same response.

A child will have a sense of how bad or good a behavior might be all on her own. If your reaction completely belies her notions your child will lose her ability to trust herself and her perceptions. She won't know what the "reality" is.

Children need to have their correct instincts affirmed.

Fury over a dish left in the sink, or even cheating on a test will leave her shaken and confused.

"I must be horrible," she will think. "I didn't mean to do anything horrible but it happened anyway...."

You want a child who thinks, "Wow, did I make a mistake. Dad is really angry about me coming home so late. I'm not usually like this, either..."

The latter child knows she's good. The former has no idea what's wrong with her.

SEEING IT IN ACTION:

Your Four-Year-Old

You've told Jenna several times to keep the paint on the paper. She's working on a plastic mat that is resting on the floor. But somehow she has consistently tended to move the paper within inches of the perimeter.

"Careful." You turn toward the oven to finish up dinner.

Turning back around a minute or so later, you see a bright streak of red tracing the edge of the paper onto the floor.

Jenna is clearly oblivious

"Jenna, you got the paint on the floor," you snap angrily. "I told you to be careful."

Jenna's eyes widened. She hadn't noticed. A second later they fill with tears. "I'm sorry," she wails.

You bend down swiftly, damp sponge in hand and

wipe off the red. The truth is the paint is water soluble and the floor is linoleum. You just can't stand messes. It's a problem for a person with children!

You take a deep breath. What does a four-year-old care about shiny clean floors? How could she understand how you feel about it? You hardly do!

Holding up the sponge you show her the red paint. "Ta dah!" you say cheerfully. Then you grow a bit more serious. "Jenna, I've told you to keep the paint on the paper. Not the floor. I know you can do it. Please be more careful. The floor is fine. Mommy just doesn't like messes."

Jenna smiles with relief, and merrily goes back to her masterpiece. After all, she's a fine artist at work.

Your Nine-Year-Old

John has always been a temperamental child. Also a self-conscious one. He's especially uncomfortable meeting and/or greeting people. He looks away. He mutters hello. It's rare that he smiles. And then sometimes he simply acts like a five-year-old. You find it very embarrassing. This you know is your problem. But you also worry. John doesn't put forth a very likeable face. You're afraid people will forever have trouble warming to him.

You've worked hard at this with him and have been making headway. He has lately been managing to look the person in the eye and smile slightly. And rather than let his nervousness spiral into babyish behavior, he's been finding it easier to quietly look at a book, or play a game.

Now, an old friend from college is due any second, and you've gently reminded John of what you expect.

You feel quite firmly that a nine-year-old should be able to muster a polite hello, even if he is feeling a bit shy.

The doorbell rings. You rush forward to embrace your friend, and then eagerly drag her into the living room to meet John.

But he clearly has other plans. He doesn't look up, he murmurs hello and then immediately starts tossing a silk pillow around, an object with which he is not allowed to play.

You feel terribly embarrassed and so begin talking busily to your friend at which point John interrupts you with a silly question.

Holding in your mounting annoyance you answer him.

But then he asks another one.

"Can I have my birthday present early? PLEASE! PRETTY PLEASE!"

He's acting like a five-year-old.

So you try very hard not to. Quietly and firmly you suggest that if he's going to be silly, he should go find something else to do.

Apologizing, you continue the visit, and when your friend leaves you go upstairs.

John is clearly waiting for a blowup. He doesn't even look at you when you walk in.

You actually feel like slapping him. Last time he behaved this way you were so distressed you told him if he kept this up no one will ever like him. But this time you hold on to yourself.

You are aware you wanted your friend to think you're a great mother and that your children are fabulous and this you know is your problem. John's behavior was annoying, but he is only nine, he is genuinely self-conscious, and more than anything else, he needs to feel that he's okay. Sometimes, as a result, he regresses.

"John, I am very disappointed that you couldn't behave with a little more self-control around Mary. She didn't get to see what a great kid you are at all."

"Well, YOU SENT ME TO MY ROOM," John cries out angrily.

"I didn't want to watch you being so silly and rude. It was making me very angry. Also frustrated. You can do better but you didn't show that at all. It's unacceptable to behave like that to guests in this house. How would you like it if your friends walked in and I didn't say hello and just started saying silly things to you?"

"That'd be okay," John insists.

"I don't think so," you counter. "No TV tonight. And the next time you behave this way it will be no TV for two nights. You have to get this behavior of yours under control."

John shrugs, "I don't care," he says softly.

You let that sit. (See technique #7.)

Your Twelve-Year-Old:

Alice was caught copying homework off a friend's paper. She'd hardly studied the night before because of a fight with a friend, and the next day, realizing she was ill prepared, talked her friend into helping her out.

But the teacher saw her and sent a note home to you requesting that you make sure Alice does her work every evening.

You are very upset both with Alice and with the implication that you should be more vigilant about your child's homework.

In fact, you are about to level all manner of punishment upon Alice, when after forcing yourself to calm down just a bit, you remember a few of your own poorly prepared days at school. They didn't happen because you were lazy, or dishonest. You had simply gotten caught up with other things, and before you knew it the next day had arrived and you were behind. It never occurred to you to offer an explanation to anyone. You'd simply done what Alice did. You copied off a friend.

Calmly, you sit down with Alice and instead of launching into a tirade about how no one will be able to trust her again and that copying homework is a dreadful and dishonest thing to do, you ask her how she feels about what happened.

"I feel sick . . ." she murmurs. "The teacher hates me now . . ."

"No she doesn't," you assure her. "But she probably is disappointed in you."

"I'm so embarrassed," Alice cries, putting both her hands over her face.

It occurs to you that you didn't need to reprimand her. She's doing a good job of it herself. In fact, she's being just a little too unforgiving of herself.

"Look, honey, you're not the first kid to come to school unprepared. I think it was probably because of your fighting with Lily last night that you didn't get it done. You know, next time instead of copying, why don't you try telling the teacher you had a problem last night and you'll have it ready the next day? Teachers have difficult evenings, too!"

Your daughter will probably be surprised by this approach. It doesn't occur to many students that teachers could understand they had a bad night. (Most can accept this as an excuse for no homework if it rarely happens.)

Your daughter may not realize that teachers, like parents, can keep things in perspective. And that so should she. In fact, doing so will help Alice keep her expectations of herself reasonable and fair.

Copying someone else's homework is wrong, and you can certainly say so, though, of course, she knows that. She's been reprimanded by her teacher. You could continue to lay on the guilt in the hopes that she will never repeat such a "sin" again, but doing so will leave her wallowing in humiliation instead of working out how not to make the mistake again.

Letting your daughter see that this behavior does not define who she is, but rather is the result of a problem, will help to make sure an episode like this does not happen again.

TECHNIQUE #16

NAME YOUR POISON

WORKS FOR: HELPING YOUR CHILD THINK TWICE ABOUT A POOR BEHAVIOR BEFORE DOING IT AS WELL AS GIVING HIM SOME CONTROL OVER AND RESPONSIBILITY FOR THE CONSEQUENCE, THUS LIMITING YOUR "BAD GUY" IMAGE.

THE TECHNIQUE

Ask your child to name an appropriate consequence for a misbehavior, making it clear that you may or may not agree but that her opinions will certainly play a part in the ultimate decision.

This can be used both to avert a probable infraction as well as after the fact. However, if you use it before the misbehavior, be sure it is for an act that both you and your child know is very commonplace for him. Otherwise you will be conveying distrust and a lack of confidence in his ability to simply do the right thing.

To thwart a typical poor behavior before it starts you might say to your child, "I want to come home and hear from the baby-sitter that you listened to her this time. You know we've had trouble with this before. What do you think the consequence should be if she reports you didn't?"

If it's after the fact, you might say, "I'm very angry that you went out with your friends after school when I specifically told you to do your homework first. There has to be a consequence for this. What do you think it should be?''

In both instances, be clear that ultimately the decision is yours. ''I want to know what you think is fair, and we'll see if I agree. If not, we'll reach a compromise.''

Don't be surprised if your child names a consequence that is a bit too harsh. She may do so in an effort to please, but you will want to make it clear that severity is not what would please you. You are more interested in good behavior.

''I think two weeks of no TV is a little steep. I'd be satisfied with one, knowing from then on you'd get your homework done first thing.''

Your child might also try and get away with a very inconsequential consequence, which, of course, you cannot allow, either. ''That seems a bit too comfortable to me,'' you might say with a smile. ''Skipping our evening checkers game one night isn't going to help you remember not to do this again. I'd say no checkers for three nights and no TV, either, would be a bit more memorable.''

Again, remember to try and use your child's suggestions as much as possible. And do, when possible, relate the punishment to the ''crime.''

WHY IT WORKS

A child will be more likely to remember a consequence that he himself has helped design before he acts, than if it was one of your choice alone.

If the poor behavior has already occurred, having

named the consequence, or at least contributed to its form, your child will be more accepting. He will not waste as much energy on being angry at the consequence as he will on his annoyance at himself for behaving poorly.

Also, allowing your child to contribute to his consequence limits the resentment he will feel for you. You have not played "the master" dispensing a punishment at will. You did not place yourself above him looking down and making proclamations. You allowed the playing field to be a bit less slanted. Not entirely level, of course. He wouldn't want that anyway. But you let him know it's not a case of being on opposing sides.

And in so doing your child will focus more on the misbehavior, than the punishment. Which is exactly what you want.

THE DEEPER MESSAGE

When you allow your child to talk with you about a consequence not only are you showing her respect but you are teaching her how to discriminate. You are teaching the relationship between actions and consequences, about making fair judgments and also about talking with others to gain a full perspective about a problem.

In arriving at a fair consequence together you are helping her see the misbehavior is not a catastrophe and that reactions to things have to be modulated. That throwing the baby out with the bath water is no solution to any problem.

SEEING IT IN ACTION:

Your Four-Year-Old

Alice simply will not behave herself at a restaurant. She throws sugar bags around, rips napkins, speaks way too loudly, and crawls under the table.

For a few months you refused to take her to any restaurant including fast-food places. But that didn't really work as it cut down on taking a break from meal planning and enjoying a nice meal with your spouse and ten-year-old.

So you decided to try again, but Alice spun out of control. You ended up leaving the restaurant before dessert, utterly furious.

It's two weeks later, Sunday evening, and you've decided to go out to a local Chinese restaurant. You are hoping against hope that Alice doesn't ruin the experience for everyone. And so you sit her down on the sofa, look at her seriously, and say, "Alice. We are all going out for Chinese food to a restaurant."

"Oh goodie!" She claps her hands.

"But, Alice, I want you to promise me that you are going to behave well this time. You'll stay in your seat. You'll use your 'inside' voice."

"Okay! Yeah!" Alice agrees readily.

"It's very important to me that you behave well. I'm going to be upset if you don't and am going to have to give you a consequence if you act badly."

"All right." Alice nods enthusiastically, hardly listening.

"So what should the consequence be?" you press on.

"Huh?" Alice asks. She's listening to you now.

"What should the consequence be if you don't behave nicely in the restaurant? I'd like to hear your idea."

"Well . . ." Alice hesitates. This is an unusual twist. What ought to happen if she does all that stuff that makes Mommy mad? "No dessert?"

"Almost," you say slowly. "But I think no dessert and no cartoon before bed."

" 'Kay . . ." Alice says.

Later that evening you enter the restaurant and Alice promptly starts playing with her glass of water.

"Alice," you say quietly. "Remember what *we* decided about dessert and TV?"

Alice immediately withdraws her hand and rests them on the table.

She makes a few wrong moves during dinner. You can tell she's working hard to control herself. You have to admonish her gently only two more times.

After dinner, she asks to go out for ice cream.

"Absolutely." You smile. "I'm proud of you."

"Dessert and TV. Right?" Alice says, clearly remembering what she herself had agreed to.

Your Nine-Year-Old

David is extremely careless with his things. He loses gloves and hats almost every week and doesn't seem to feel much remorse. And if he doesn't actually lose them, he leaves them places, so that half the week his hands and ears are freezing. This does not seem to influence his behavior at all, however.

Finally, you can no longer abide the idea of him without gloves or hat in the freezing cold weather. Nor can you tolerate all that wasted money.

So you sit him down.

"This losing of gloves and hats has got to stop," you inform him.

"I don't care about that," he says irritably.

"Well, I care," you respond evenly. "If you do it again, there's going to have to be a consequence. I don't want you walking around without a hat and gloves and I'm tired of wasting money. There's no reason why you can't hang on to these things. What do you think a fair consequence would be if you come home without your stuff again?"

David shrugs, purposefully trying to minimize the situation. "I don't know. No TV tonight?"

"Nope, I'm tired of that. Besides, you don't watch much. How about you dig into your money box and pay me back for this last pair of gloves and the hat if you lose them?

"But I'm saving for a snowboard!" David cries out. "That's too much!"

"What wouldn't be?" you ask pleasantly.

"A dollar," David shrugs.

"A dollar for each item," you counter. "That's two dollars for the gloves and one for the hat. Agreed?"

"Okay," David says begrudgingly. "All right."

The next day he walks in the door with both gloves but missing his hat.

"Where's your hat?" you ask with irritation.

"It's in my bag. It's not that cold, but I didn't want to lose it," David grouses good-naturedly.

Your Twelve-Year-Old

Jessica has matured a little early and is starting to act a bit too old for her age. She's wearing makeup, talking about boys nonstop, and increasingly becoming more secretive. It's worrying you tremendously. You don't want this to get out of hand, you want her to be cautious, but you don't want to sit on her, either. You're afraid that tactic will bring a full-scale rebellion.

So far you've been quietly setting firm but reasonable rules. She has to be home from school at a particular time and get her homework done before any socializing. When she does go out, you need to know who with, and if she sleeps at a friend's house, you want to know what the plans are for the evening and that a parent will be supervising.

Tonight, however, you are furious. Jessica told you she'd be at her friend Priscilla's for dinner. But Priscilla called an hour ago clearly unaware that Jessica had claimed to have plans with her. You've been worried sick, and now Jessica has just walked in the door. You confront her with what you have learned.

Jessica is silent. There are tears in her eyes, but you feel unmoved. You are too furious.

"You know perfectly well I have always insisted that you tell me what you're doing. I would not stand in your way unnecessarily."

"But . . . but . . ." Jessica begins, clearly miserable, "I ran into Linda and I . . ."

"You were not with Linda," you insist. "I called to see if she knew where you were and she did not."

Jessica hangs her head. "I met Jack."

''Who's Jack?'' you snap.

''This boy. I had dinner with him at Leo's for pizza. He's in the eighth grade and . . .''

This you can tell is true. You caught a whiff of her pizza breath a moment ago.

''Why didn't you tell me?'' you persist.

''I didn't think you'd let me go.'' Jessica sighed. ''I'm sorry.''

''I might have, I might not have,'' you concur. ''But that's no reason to lie. Did it occur to you that it might be dangerous for you to meet someone without anyone else knowing where you are?''

Jessica remains silent.

''Did you forget the rule I have about always letting me know what's up?'' You are fuming.

''I guess so,'' Jessica answers quietly.

''This was a terrible thing you did. I'm extremely angry. Not about the fact that you had a date. It's that you lied. It's that I knew nothing about it or Jack. This cannot happen again. It has to stop right here. There's going to be a consequence.''

''What?'' Jessica says unhappily, flopping into a chair.

You pull one up next to her. ''I don't quite know,'' you respond. ''What do you think?''

''I don't know. Ground me for a month or something . . .'' she says guiltily.

You hesitate. You're tempted. But it does seem a little steep. This is her first offense.

''Well, I appreciate your approach,'' you say seriously. ''But this is the first time to my knowledge that you've lied to me. I think the grounding is a good idea, but two weeks would satisfy me.''

Jessica looks up at you impressed.

"Jessica, I expect this is never going to happen again. If there's something you want to do that you think I'll disapprove of, either don't do it or let's discuss it. You're not a mind reader. You don't know what I'd say. And anyway, maybe we can compromise."

Jessica nods with a sad smile and goes upstairs.

You can tell you caught her attention. She heard what you were saying. She didn't get caught up with screaming "No fair!" to the consequence.

You treated her like a mature person, which is what she is struggling to be . . . in her still childlike way.

Time-Outs Are Simply a Private Matter

WORKS FOR: MISBEHAVIOR OF ANY KIND—REFUSAL TO COOPERATE—ANNOYING BEHAVIOR.

THE TECHNIQUE

The most important component of a time-out is that the child receives no social attention. Whether he is asked to sit in a quiet place near others, or sent to his room or another appropriate place, the point is, he needs to be left alone.

There are, however, two ways to give a time out. Which you choose will depend on the nature of the problem behavior. In both cases, however, be sure to explain the purpose of the timeout, and to make it clear you *both* need a break.

If the child is simply being disruptive and annoying, perhaps laughing too loudly, or chasing a younger sibling, or unable to stop whining, you would first warn him that if he doesn't stop he is going to get a time-out. If he continues to misbehave, you would send him to his room until he feels able to stop the misbehavior. "Okay. I warned you. Now, please go to your room and stay there until you think you can come back out and behave reasonably. I'm getting angry and I don't want to lose my temper.'' You are in essence putting your child in command of the time-out.

In an instance where your child commits an action that is inappropriate or breaks a rule, such as hitting a sibling, or speaking rudely, the time-out would have to take on another dimension. Specifically, the parameters are your call. ''What you have just said to me is unacceptable. Go to your room for fifteen minutes and collect yourself. If there's something bothering you, perhaps you'll be able to tell me what it is in a nicer way when the time is up. I'm too annoyed to listen to you right now anyway. You may come downstairs in fifteen minutes. I'll tell you when that is'' (the younger child), or ''You may come downstairs in thirty minutes'' (the older child).

In either case it isn't necessary to close a door. That can frighten a child, especially a young one. And while there is some debate over whether or not a child should be assigned a task (writing an essay about why he shouldn't have done what he did) this, most experts and parents agree, defeats the purpose of the time-out. It simply requires too much of your attention!

Finally, there is the issue of what happens if your child won't go. If the child is very young you can probably carry him upstairs or into a room. You might be tempted to insist that he sit down while you wait outside the room as a sort of gatekeeper. This is problematic, however, because once again you are giving him your attention. The entire fifteen minutes will be spent with the two of you locked in battle. That can be a very interesting ''social interaction'' for your child!

It would be much wiser to simply say, ''Well, I can't

make you go. But if you don't, there will be no TV tonight.'' If you choose something that would clearly make his life uncomfortable he is far more likely to trade it for fifteen minutes on his own. You will also be giving him a chance to control his own destiny. Even though neither choice is a party, he will feel, at least, like co-captain of his own ship.

Finally, with younger children the phrase ''time-out'' is acceptable. They read it as a consequence, but it doesn't sound terribly ominous. An older child, however, doesn't want to hear the phrase. He will consider it too babyish. You need to describe the consequence. Not la-bel it. ''I want you to remove yourself from where I am, because I'm angry and it's unpleasant with you here. We'll talk later.''

WHY IT WORKS

Time-outs work because they are a very clear message. If a child is going to be annoying, or misbehave, his presence is simply not desirable. He is being socially unacceptable, and so he will not be allowed to be social. It's actually an extremely tidy consequence for poor be-havior!

It also works because it is an opportunity to both draw immediate dramatic attention to what has just happened, and to end the possibility of things going from bad to worse. This will keep you from engaging in an extended battle of wills with your child, and will relieve your child of his natural desire to ''win.'' You're not there, and so there can be no argument. He can take the time to break the tension inside himself that inspired the poor behavior, and you can calm your nerves and temper by interrupting your interaction with your child.

THE DEEPER MESSAGE

You want your child to gain control of himself. This is not simply a consequence. It's an opportunity for him to take a deep breath and settle himself down. And in some cases, for you to do the same. This is an example of good modeling (see technique #8). But it is also an important message about the way *you* wish to be treated. You do not want to be around a person who is exhibiting disrespect for you or your wishes. You are perfectly happy to be around him, and even to discuss a bad feeling, but he has to do it in a civilized fashion. Otherwise, you're not interested.

Finally, you are telegraphing your confidence that the two of you can be together in a terrific way, and that you don't want to scream, fuss, or coerce to get there.

You want both of you to take responsibility for a peaceful time.

SEEING IT IN ACTION

Your Four-Year-Old

You are having an important conversation on the phone with a dear friend, when your four-year-old, as usual, comes running over, urgency streaming from every pore.

"Mommy, Mommy, I have to tell you something."

You put your hand up and whisper, "Wait a minute, honey. I'll be off in a few minutes."

"But Mommy, Mommy, you have to come. This thing I have to show you that . . ."

You tell your friend to hang on one moment and then turn to your son, "Is anything wrong?"

"No, but . . ." he plows forward.

"Then I'll come look in a few minutes, right now I'm on the phone."

You turn back to your conversation, but your son promptly steps up his decibels. "Mommy, PLEASE, Mommy I want . . ."

"You're getting a time-out if you don't stop this right now," you snap. "I will talk to you later, but right now you are interrupting me and it's making me angry."

"But, Mommy . . ." He's tugging on your sleeve now.

"That's it," you say matter-of-factly. You ask your friend to hang on and then taking your son by his hand you lead him to his room. "You will sit here until you think you can let me finish my conversation. If you think you can stop talking to me until I'm through, you may come out."

"NO!!! he shrieks. "I don't want a time-out!"

"Fine," you say quietly. "Don't bother me while I'm on the phone. I will talk to you as soon as I am off." And then turn around and walk out of his room.

Chances are he will leave you be.

If he doesn't, you can simply say, "Either you stay in your room until you can let me finish my conversation, or you can skip cartoons for three mornings. Your choice."

Your Nine-Year-Old

Nine-year-old Walter has a major love/hate relationship with his little brother Ben. One moment it's as if *not* being with him would make it difficult to breathe. But shortly thereafter he can become so annoyed by his brother's antics that he can't get to his room fast enough to hide.

Walter is also a quick-tempered, volatile personality and is given to hitting his younger brother. Lately, in fact, Walter's been slapping Ben's head. A light smack on the behind doesn't get you riled. But the head is something altogether different and you've already told him twice to stop it, explaining the dangers.

But now, Ben has just walked into the playroom where Walter is now watching TV, unadvisedly gripping one of Walter's toys. He receives a smack on the head.

"That's it," you say, standing up abruptly to face Walter. "Time-out upstairs. I've explained that hitting someone on the head is not allowed. I'm very upset with you. I don't want you coming back down for half an hour."

"He had my toy!" Walter protests indignantly.

"Yes, and maybe he found it in the hallway or the kitchen or even if he did take it from your bedroom, he does not deserve a slap on the head. Call me instead. Or ask him to give it to you immediately. Now go."

"I don't want to," he wails.

"I know that. Next time you might remember not to hit him like that. "GO!"

"I won't," he insists, folding his arms across his chest.

"If you don't go now there will be no TV for five days, and I will have to cancel your play date with Bill this afternoon, which I would hate to do." You say this calmly and with great solemn resolve. Then, you leave the room. (A child will often find it easier to back down without an audience.)

Ben stands up, grumbling, and walks out.

But half an hour later you find him upstairs reading a book.

"You can come down now," you say.

"Okay . . ." he says quietly. Not in a defeated way, either. It's clear his mind has traveled elsewhere. That's all. He got what he deserves. He knows that. But you broke the tug-of-war, while at the same time giving him a choice. He'll know that, too.

It'll help cool him down.

Your Twelve-Year-Old

You have just asked for the second time that Peter go clean up his room, but he isn't doing it. He would rather watch television. Ordinarily you wouldn't insist but you're expecting company. You explain this to him for the second time. He still isn't moving and so you flip off the television set.

"You stink," he says loudly.

This infuriates you. You know this kind of challenge is typical of the age, but it is unacceptable to you. Peter's been behaving this way more and more, and you want it to stop.

"I want your room cleaned now, and then I don't want to see your face down here until company comes. You may not speak to me this way. If you're upset about something having to do with me or anything else, tell me. But you are not allowed to say such rude things."

"Okay, I'm sorry," he says, getting up to flick the TV back on. "I'll clean up as soon as this is over."

"No. Now," you respond, stopping him cold. "Let's not turn this into a whole scene. Go up and clean your room, and stay there. I'm tired of the way you've been behaving and I think we both need time to cool off. I know I do."

"This place is like a prison," he mutters as he passes you by on the way upstairs.

That's fine. So he gets the last word. Let him save face (see technique #5). You took a strong stand and he will want to maintain some dignity in the face of what he perceives is "your win."

TECHNIQUE #18

If He Makes the Bed, Let Him Lie in It

WORKS FOR: WHEN YOUR CHILD REFUSES TO COMPLETE HIS SCHOOLWORK IN A TIMELY FASHION, LISTEN TO YOUR ADVICE ABOUT POSITIVE SOCIAL BEHAVIOR, TURNS DOWN YOUR ASSISTANCE IN LONG-TERM SCHOOL PROJECTS AND YOU CAN SEE HE'S FALLING BEHIND, LIES DESPITE YOUR WARNINGS ABOUT NOT DOING SO, AND MORE . . .

THE TECHNIQUE

There is everything to be gained from offering your child guidance with life skills as well as reminders of his responsibilities. But it is critical to leave the primary accountability for his actions in his hands, and to allow him to experience the logical consequences of his both positive and negative behaviors.

If your child refuses to respond to your admonishment that there is little time left to finish his book report, or that continual bossy behavior will lose him friends, then it is important to step back. He needs to experience what he has wrought, unfettered by an argument with you. And you have to convince yourself that allowing him "to reap what he sows" is a necessary component of parenting. Ultimately, his behavior can only be legislated by him. The sooner you let him take responsibility for it, the faster he will learn how to be his own best support.

However, when your child does fall on his face, adhere to one cardinal rule: No direct "I told you sos." A gentle reiteration of what has to happen in the future will do. "Your science experiment is coming up in two weeks. After you're finished with this last project, I'll help you plan how to get it done on time."

WHY IT WORKS

The goal is to help your child take responsibility for his own actions and to use his own initiative to meet life's challenges.

When you tangle endlessly with your child about what will happen if he continues to behave in a particular way, you are turning his attention to winning a battle with you, rather than the possible consequences of what he is doing.

When your child experiences the problems he himself has produced he will be forced to recognize how it happened. If you were to step in constantly and save him from himself, he would never see the world or himself realistically.

Sometimes people need to feel the full negative impact of their choices in order to make better more constructive ones. Constant battles with your child that result in him just barely squeaking by will give him a false impression of how things get done and little sense of personal accomplishment; it will also leave him utterly dependent on you. Allowing him to fall on his face will illustrate very clearly what he needs to do, and what will happen if he doesn't.

THE DEEPER MESSAGE

Your child has to learn to stand on his own.

He also needs to separate from you.

And you him.

It is extremely painful for parents to watch their children make mistakes that will cause them embarrassment or unhappiness. But by allowing them to stumble you are not only teaching them about real life, you are making a statement about your connection with them:

You love your child, you want to help him, but in the end you are separate people. If he makes a mistake, it is his. You will not be sucked into it, or take responsibility for it. When you can calmly look at what's happened and say, "Well, I guess next time you will have to prepare a little differently for a test," without fury or any other intense emotion, you are telling your child, "Hey, this is your life."

Ironically, in the end you will have helped him manage it better than had you kept at him relentlessly until out of sheer exhaustion he succumbed to your entreaties. And in so doing you will improve the dynamics of your relationships with him.

SEEING IT IN ACTION:

Your Four-Year-Old

Harrison is very bossy. He is a friendly child, happy and enthusiastic, but when he wants to do something in a particular way he refuses to bend. Two of his friends in particular have been having trouble with Harrison because of his relentlessness and you have tried to step in. But Harrison will have none of it.

You've tried pulling him aside to explain he needs to let his friend Charlie have a turn at the computer, or that Eric doesn't want to play superheroes and maybe he can find some other thing to do. But Harrison, with a look of annoyance, has consistently insisted, ''No. This is OKAY . . .''

You could see he was headed for trouble.

Sure enough you have just gotten a phone call from Charlie's mom, apologizing for canceling a date with Harrison. ''Charlie doesn't want to come,'' she explains gently. ''He seems to feel Harrison won't let him do anything at your house that he wants to do . . .''

You assure her that Charlie's perception is largely accurate and that you will try and work this through with Harrison.

Walking into the playroom, you see Harrison look up from his book. ''Charlie here yet?'' he asks happily.

It breaks your heart.

''Charlie's not coming,'' you say gently, sitting down next to him.

''Why not?'' Harrison cries out. ''I want to play with him!''

''Well,'' you say, careful to sound sympathetic and not triumphant, ''Charlie's mommy told me Charlie doesn't want to come because you don't let him do things he wants to do. You need to have things your way too much . . .''

''NO I DON'T!'' Harrison cries out indignantly.

''Well, maybe not all the time,'' you say, ''but you

do tell him what to do a lot. He doesn't like that.''

"Okay, well this time he could do what he wants,'' Harrison almost whimpers. "He can . . . call him.''

"I'm not going to call him right now, sweetie, because I think he's probably busy. But I think in a day or two we can call again and see if he'd like to try another play date. I'm sure he will.''

"Okay.'' Harrison shrugs sadly. "So who can I play with today?''

"I think maybe you will just have to play with your toys and I'll play a game with you a little later . . .''

Harrison starts to cry. "I want a play date!''

"You'll have another play date soon,'' you assure him. "And I know next time you'll let your friends tell you what they'd like to do. Right?!''

"Right . . .'' Harrison sighs begrudgingly.

Your Nine-Year-Old

Steven resists doing homework. Long-term projects, however, have become the bane of both of your existences. He can't seem to figure out how to break up the components of an assignment so that he gets a little done each day, and no matter what you say he rejects your advice. It's a mad rush at the end. For both of you.

Each time a book report, science experiment, or history project is due you have to keep on top of every single stage, pushing and prodding him to go through the paces necessary to complete the work. By the time the project is due, the two of you aren't talking, half of it has been done by you, and the night before is a flurry of ridiculous activity.

This you realize has to stop. And now.

"I'll do it!" Steven snaps at you this afternoon, five days before a diorama and one-page report is due on a significant historical event from World War II.

"But you need to at least choose the event and collect materials and a book or two on the subject!" you exclaim, bewildered by his nonchalant attitude toward the project.

"Okay, I WILL!" he cries out with exasperation. "I just want to finish building this model," he adds, barely looking up from the Challenger model he is now constructing.

You want to simply remove the model from his room. You want to drag your son to his desk. But this time you decide maybe you've done enough.

"Fine," you say with a smile. "If you need any help let me know. You've got a lot of work ahead of you." And then you exit Steven's room.

A day goes by and you notice Steven has done nothing.

Then another.

You decide, and quite rightly, there is no need to sit completely silently by while he wastes his time. A gentle reminder would be okay, and help you feel less guilty when the inevitable occurs. You wander into Steven's room.

"Gotten anything done on your project, honey? It's due the day after tomorrow, isn't it?"

"I don't know what event to pick," Steven says matter-of-factly as if now that he's explained that, you'll take over.

"Well, I have a few books on World War Two downstairs. Why don't you pick one, and select a battle or a key meeting between world leaders."

"Which one?" Steven says, persisting in his desire for you to do more than your share.

"Come with me," you say with a smile. He follows you downstairs, you pull a book off a shelf and hand it to him. "Skim this. Look at the pictures. Pick something that looks interesting yourself. We can discuss what you need to do after."

About ten minutes later Steven reappears with the book. "The Battle of the Bulge," he says. "I guess I need a shoe box, construction paper . . . stuff like that."

"I'll get you the box from my room." You nod. "The other things I think you have. You could make soldiers out of your brother's Play-Doh or use your Lego men. And don't you need something for . . ."

"I'll do it later," Steven nods.

"Are you going to work on the paper first?" you ask, feeling your body growing tense.

"Yeah, after dinner," Steven replies as he follows you to your room. You hand him the box and smile.

"Okay," you respond, knowing there is no way the project is going to be done.

The next day you notice that Steven has started the diorama.

You see no signs of a composition paper on his desk.

That evening you wander by his room and Steven is just finishing his math homework. "So, is everything ready?" you ask. It's actually been a long workday for you and you're exhausted.

Suddenly tears spring to Steven's eyes. "I don't know what to do first?!" He sighs heavily. "Can you help me?"

You check your watch. You'd intended to go to bed in half an hour. You're about to say "okay," when you remind yourself that if not for you this scene would have happened five times already this year. That maybe this feeling of desperation, of having made a big mistake, is exactly what Steven needs to stop the pattern.

"You know, honey, I've been telling you all week to get started and you've argued with me or ignored me each time. It's late, you shouldn't be working right now anyway, and I'm going to sleep. I'm afraid you are going to have to just go to school tomorrow and tell the teacher you didn't do it on time. She'll probably lower your grade, and have a thing or two to say to you, but I'm afraid that's what you're stuck with."

"But I can't go into school without it!" Steven cries out.

"Yes you can," you assure him. "It isn't good, but maybe this will help you remember next time to get started early. You're not the first student to put something off too long and you won't be the last." (Be careful not to blow this out of proportion. See technique #15.)

"I hate you!" Steven snaps.

"I think you're angry at yourself," you respond calmly and then close the door behind you.

You wake up at two in the morning and take a peek in his room. A partial essay is on Steven's desk. The diorama is messy and incomplete. And Steven is sprawled on top of his bed fast asleep.

You have a feeling this is not going to happen again.

Your Twelve-Year-Old

Maggie wants to be on the sixth grade baseball team. She's not terribly athletic, but she likes the game anyway. And she has determined that since her friends are all planning to try out she wants to as well. It will be, she's sure, great fun.

You know, however, that she needs to practice for the big day. You've been telling her this for the last three weeks. But she won't listen. Though she'll go out and play a game with her pals, she does not have the patience to allow you to drill her in batting and catching.

You can smell a disaster coming a mile away. There are only a few days left and you decide to put it clearly on the line one more time. Standing at Maggie's bedroom door you pause before speaking. She's reading a book and looks very sweet.

"Maggie," you interrupt her gently. "You know that baseball tryout is in a few days. Want to go out and practice?"

"Not right now. I'll be okay," she says contentedly.

You go for broke this time. "Honey, I don't think you're ready. I have a feeling the other kids trying out are more consistent hitters. Let's make sure you've got a little more skill under your belt."

"Later," Maggie says, hardly looking up.

"Okay," you say. And then you close the door.

You wait for her to ask, and she doesn't.

And so the day arrives and Maggie flies off to school, cheerful as ever, only to return, as you expected, very deflated, not to mention angry.

She slams the front door, runs upstairs, and screams out, "I hate everybody!" which you suspect is a loose translation for "I hate the mistake I made . . ."

You wait a moment and then go upstairs to find her lying on her bed crying.

"What happened?" you ask gently.

"I was horrible . . ." she sobs.

"That must have felt bad," you say, careful to avoid an I told you so.

"I was the worst one . . ."

"You'll get better. There will be other tryouts," you murmur.

"But I'm so embarrassed . . ." Maggie continues pitifully.

"I guess you are, but really, I'm sure no one was paying half as much attention to you as you think they were. They were far more worried about their own game . . ."

Maggie continues to bury her head in the pillow, quieting down a bit.

And so you make your point, indirectly.

"You'll practice this year, and if you want to try out again next year, you'll be ready."

Maggie doesn't argue.

TECHNIQUE #19

JUST BE THERE

WORKS FOR: YOUR CHILD'S HURT FEELINGS, SENSE OF LOSS, DISAPPOINTMENT, BROKEN HEART, BAD DAY, FEELINGS OF REJECTION, AND MORE . . .

THE TECHNIQUE

Comfort with your presence, not your words. If your child arrives home from school, deflated and upset, don't pounce on him with questions and advice. Let him feel what he needs to feel. Offer him a snack, or simply sit next to him while he broods, cries, or talks incessantly in an effort to get it all out.

You can, of course, speak, but keep words to a minimum. "That hurts," or "I can see why you're so sad," are fine, reflective statements that do not require your child to move from where he is at. Just be there, sharing the moment. Don't intrude on his thoughts. Allow him his space but by your gestures show him you understand and are right beside him. And if it's something you're both upset about, for instance the loss of a pet, don't be afraid to show him you are hurting, too.

Only after you see that he has calmed down, or notice that he seems interested in something other than his pain, should you try and advise or offer concrete suggestions.

You might try, "Maybe we could talk about what to do next time your friends treat you that way . . ."

Do keep in mind, however, there are some children who when terribly upset, will insist they don't want you in the room. Listen to them and leave. But make it clear you are nearby, that you are removing yourself only physically, not emotionally. "Okay. But I'll be downstairs in the kitchen if you need me," will let him know that while you will let him alone, in a much deeper sense, he will never *be* alone.

Finally, with older children, you might have an opportunity to talk about the importance of accepting a bad feeling. Take advantage of the moment. Teaching a child not to hide from pain is an extremely important gift.

WHY IT WORKS

Sometimes words, no matter how carefully chosen, or filled with wisdom, are more of a hindrance than help. They get in the way of the feeling. They interrupt it, or hurry it, or attempt to transform it "before it's time."

In fact, trying to attack a painful feeling with reason, or even simply to analyze it in detail, could push your child away. He may need to hang on to the feeling, and his sense that you want to banish it could alienate him. Also he may for a time *not want* to include you in on it because if he does you might criticize him. Or want to get uncomfortably close to him. The truth is, only by facing a negative feeling head-on, and experiencing its pain, can one begin to healthfully move past it. There is a time for wise words and new perspectives but they need to be introduced when your child is ready to hear and use them. Otherwise, they will leave him feeling misunderstood and lonely.

Clearly, you should not allow a child to sit and ruminate over a problem for an extended period of time without interceding with some comforting words to draw him out followed up by some parental wisdom. But by waiting a respectful amount of time (you could let the entire afternoon go by) you will be giving your child what he needs.

Permission to feel.

He will climb out of this painful spot because he won't want to stay there. The desire to feel better will make him available to whatever you can give. So hang on to yourself. Parents often, in an effort to make themselves feel better (watching a child in pain can be awful) move in too fast with "fix-its." Don't do it.

This JUST BE THERE technique will work because it's timed according to your child's clock. Not yours.

THE DEEPER MESSAGE

Your child will know he is not alone. Nor is he abandoned. He will feel hugely comforted by the notion that he is understood without him having to say a word.

He will also receive the message that he doesn't have to "be" any particular way. That he doesn't have to hide his feelings or make you "happy" or "relieved" by behaving in a way he simply doesn't feel. You will be telling him he has a right to his feelings. He doesn't have to change them for your sake. He doesn't have to protect you from them. You are strong enough to withstand what he has to give.

Again, you are in control.

So he doesn't have to be. Not every minute, anyway.

SEEING IT IN ACTION:

Your Five-Year-Old

Your five-year-old has two friends over for a play date and at first everything is going well. They are each, respectively, Batman, Robin, and Spiderman, and have caught an enormous amount of "bad guys."

But suddenly you hear a rift forming. It seems that Batman and Robin, played by the friends, have decided that Spiderman is not "one of them." In fact, he needs to be chased and placed in jail.

You are in your downstairs office hoping against hope that the three of them can resolve this fracture. That your son will somehow find a way to imagine himself back on their side.

But though you hear him put up a valiant effort, the other two are having none of it. Seconds later he runs upstairs and slams his bedroom door.

After making sure the other two are safely and quietly playing with superhero figures, you open your son's door where you find him, arms crossed, glaring tearfully at the wall.

"Honey, what happened . . ." you say.

"I hate them . . ." he cries out, bursting into tears. "They wouldn't let me be on their side!"

"Hmm . . ." You nod. "That must feel bad . . ."

"It does . . ." he says, still crying. He suddenly hurls the figure he is now clutching in his hand against the wall and looks at you defiantly as if to challenge you to admonish him.

You do nothing but look at him sympathetically. "Feeling left out is upsetting . . ." you say softly.

He nods, going back to crossing his arms tightly against his chest.

You sit there quietly with him, your hand resting comfortingly on his knee for a few moments.

Finally, he stands up and begins pacing around his room.

This is an indication that he may be ready to put this anger and upset aside, and instead do something. The problem is he doesn't know what.

"Would you like to go downstairs?" you ask.

"I dunno," he replies, though you can tell he would.

"How about we both go downstairs, and I'll see if I can help straighten things out. How about that? I don't think they meant to hurt your feelings. All of you are friends, after all."

He shrugs, you stand up and he follows you downstairs.

Upon entering the playroom both children look up at you a little warily. "Why don't you guys do something you can all help each other with?" You point to the blocks. "Why not build a fortress?" Then add, to no one in particular, "Making someone into a bad guy can hurt a person's feelings. So let's do this project all on the same team. Okay?"

Smile and then leave. You'll have made your point, and your son will feel protected and understood.

Your Eight-Year-Old

Your son was really looking forward to a camping trip with his friends and their fathers this coming Saturday night. But it's now Friday night, he's running a fever, and you've just found out he has strep throat. Clearly he can't go, and, of course, he is going to be crushed as he was hoping he'd be better in a matter of hours.

Slowly you walk upstairs and into his room where your son is now watching television. "Hi," he calls out cheerfully. "I think I'm feeling better."

"Good," you say softly, "that's probably the Tylenol." You sit down on the corner of his bed. "Listen, honey, the doctor just called and it seems you have strep." You let that sink in for a moment. You're not sure but you think you can see he's putting two and two together on his own. "I'm afraid the camping trip is out. You'll do that another time. . . ."

"NO!" he shouts, tears instantly running down his cheeks. "We've been planning this. I'm going. That's it!"

"Sweetie, you can't go," you repeat. "I know you feel disappointed."

"Daddy will let me," he insists, banging his fist on the blanket."

"Well, Daddy will go with you again some other time, but he's not going to let you go tomorrow."

At this point your son is shaking with frustration and disappointment. "I hate you!" he cries out.

You nod and sit there quietly looking at him. "You hate the fact that you're sick," you say sympathetically.

"No. I hate you!" he shrieks in frustration.

"I'm not letting you go." You nod. "I know it wouldn't be good for you."

"Go away," he demands. "Just go away."

"Okay, I will, but I'll just be in my room. If you want me you can call me. Getting a disappointment like this is awful. I know that." Then you stand up and walk out.

You putter around your room, making it clear that you are nearby and that you don't want to be far away from him.

After a while you open up his door, to find him lying on his bed, TV off, staring at the ceiling. "Can I come in?" you ask.

He doesn't answer, which you read as a "yes."

Quietly, you enter and sit down on his bed.

"Sometimes life can be really rotten," you say.

Your son looks at you and sighs.

"I'll rent a great tape for tomorrow night . . ." you offer. "I know it's not a camping trip, but it's a little something anyway."

"I don't want a tape," he grumbles.

And you don't argue. He isn't ready to be comforted, and so you just nod.

Later that evening, he wanders into the living room and says, "How about *Dumb and Dumber*?"

Your Twelve-Year-Old:

Your twelve-year-old daughter has been secretly "in love" for the last three weeks with a fourteen-year-old boy who she has just spotted with an "older girl." She is now lying on the living room couch, sobbing.

You sit down in the club chair and silently watch her.

Finally, she looks up with a tearstained face. "What am I going to do?" she cries out.

This sounds like she might want some advice, but it may be a rhetorical question. You decide to take a chance and literally answer by describing the principle behind this technique. "You're going to feel bad, until you don't feel bad anymore," you say simply. "That's it."

"But it hurts so much," she says sniffling. "You wouldn't understand."

"Well, it's true I'm not inside your skin," you admit, "but most everyone knows how it feels to be a little brokenhearted."

"I'll never get over it." She sighs.

"It can feel that way." You nod. It seems as if she's ready to talk and so you add, "But you will."

"How?" she asks ruefully.

"With time, and other guys," you answer simply. "You just may have to sit with the bad feeling for a while until it fades on its own. Unfortunately there's no easy way to feel hurt. You can't run away from it because it's there and it'll just come out in other ways."

"What do you mean?" she asks.

"You may be bad tempered with friends, or not concentrate at school," you explain. "It's better just to have the honest feeling. If you don't fight it, after a while it'll just get tired and then start to fade."

She nods and sighs, clearly giving into the heartbreak once again. Which is very brave, and exactly what she needs to do.

RESPECT THEIR THOUGHTS

*WORKS FOR: BUILDING THEIR SENSE OF SELF-WORTH,
AND ABILITY TO COMFORTABLY RESPECT YOU*

THE TECHNIQUE

When you take a position on a particular matter, explain yourself. ''I do not want you wearing jeans with holes at the knees to school. I think it's disrespectful to the class and teacher. It's inappropriate attire for school.''

Then, if your child feels differently, hear him out. ''But everyone wears these kinds of jeans! Tomorrow when my class sings a song at assembly I'll wear my nice corduroys.''

Listen with an open mind. If you feel swayed, say so. ''All right, that sounds fair.''

If you don't, explain why not. ''When I picked you up from the school the other day most kids were dressed very neatly. Torn jeans are for the weekend.''

And then do not allow the conversation to degenerate into a marathon hour debate. ''I hear what you're saying. If you like torn jeans, wear them. But at appropriate times. I do not feel the classroom is the correct place.

When you get home from school you can wear whatever
you want.''

WHY IT WORKS

No one likes to feel dismissed. It's far worse than not
getting one's way. The former is very disrespectful and
hurtful. The latter is simply upsetting.

When you explain a position to your child, you are
telling him he has a right to know why you feel and
think the way you do. When you listen to his thoughts,
you are telling him that his views matter. There is a
genuine communication taking place that is far more important, in the long run, than the actual issue up for
debate.

Your child will sense your willingness to hear him
out, and likely feel less combative and angry. This is so
especially if in doing so you are able to express your
understanding of his stand, and even budge a bit on
yours! His ability to back down from a staunch position
will be heightened by your willingness to consider what
he thinks.

True parental authority does not come from saying,
"Do it because I say so." It comes from conveying respect for your children without being manipulated by
them. You will be teaching them how to return the respect in kind.

THE DEEPER MESSAGE

Anytime you explain yourself or welcome the thoughts
of your child, you are encouraging her to think for her-

self. You are conveying your faith in her ability to assess, reason, and educate and your desire to let her do so. You are telling her that she has the right to express herself and deserves "a hearing."

Built into this interchange is your acceptance that *both* of you may have something to learn. That remaining open and considering different points of view is the best way to resolve a problem.

However, by setting a limit, so that you are not arguing ad infinitum, you are also maintaining control. You want your child to see that his opinions count, but that you are still the one in charge.

The key is to reach a decision with more than one view in mind. If you can communicate your willingness to do this, then you are telling your child that thinking for himself is a worthwhile endeavor.

Who he is and what he thinks matters.

SEEING IT IN ACTION:

Your-Four-Year-Old

It's thirty degrees out and Katherine doesn't want to put on her winter coat. She's insisting that her lightweight parka is fine. "I want this coat," she cries out. "I hate my other coat!"

There's no way she can go out so inadequately dressed and so you have to bite back the words, "I DON'T CARE! PUT IT ON ANYWAY!" You manage to control yourself, and instead say, "It's extremely cold out, Katherine. This coat you want to wear won't keep you warm. Your heavier coat will. Why don't you like it?''

"Because it makes me feel tight." She's starting to sob now.

"You mean it's too small?" you ask incredulously. "I just bought it!"

"No, I mean it's hard. It's stiff." She shudders.

You pick up the coat and move the arms around. It's true it's not particularly cushy. There is a rigid quality to it. But then lots of kids wear this brand.

You hesitate, knowing Katherine has an issue about the way things feel.

"Maybe I can return it," you say slowly. "But you still can't go out like that. Here's what we're going to do. Put on a sweatshirt under this coat and we'll bundle you up with a scarf."

"Good." Katherine nods, eyeing the winter coat angrily. "No more of that coat. I'll be warm another way."

You smile. You heard her and found a solution, while she clearly understood why she had to compromise. Had you skipped the part about why she has to bundle up and been unwilling to find her something more comfortable you would likely have stayed indoors or found yourself outdoors with a squirming heathen.

Your Nine-Year-Old

It's breakfast time and Jarad wants a peanut butter sandwich.

You have always been a rather traditional person and so this suggestion doesn't sit well with you. "That's a lunch food," you answer. "You can have cereal or waffles this morning."

"But I don't want cereal or waffles," Jarad insists. "Why do I have to have that? I want a peanut butter sandwich."

"It's not good for you in the morning," you answer, floundering a bit. You don't like this argument. It's not making a lot of sense. "It's too . . . heavy."

"My teacher says peanut butter has a lot of protein and that it's a nutritious food anytime . . ." Jarad's voice is louder now.

You're about to insist he drop it, when it occurs to you that he does have a point, and you, in fact, don't.

"You know something," you say slowly. "Your teacher is right. It is good for you. I'm probably being silly. If you want peanut butter you can have it. But can you have it on toast?"

"An English muffin," Jarad counters.

"Sold," you say.

Jarad grins, clearly feeling proud as he walks to the cabinet and pulls out the jar. He stated his case, and he won. He even gave you a little something in return.

You avoided a power struggle, taught your son the value of independent thinking, and modeled (see technique #13) how to back off an argument with grace.

Your Twelve-Year-Old

Mira wants to stay out late with two of her friends next Friday night. Not only do you think she's too young, but you are not comfortable with the two friends with whom she has started to spend a great deal of time. They seem nice enough, but they also do not, you believe, have proper supervision at home.

"We're just going to go to the pizza place and then

hang out by the middle school for a little while," Mira insists.

"I'm sorry." You shake your head. "Pizza and then come home. It gets dark earlier now, there's a rough crowd who sometimes comes around that school, and to be honest, Mira, I think Lucy and Kate are allowed to do things well beyond their years."

"Well, you're treating me like a baby," Mira cries out with exasperation. "I'm so embarrassed!"

"I don't think I'm treating you like a baby," you say quietly.

"I want to be with my friends," Mira persists.

"You may have pizza with them, but then you have to come home, and I don't care what you tell them. You can get around feeling embarrassed. Blame it on us. Say we're strict, you don't like it, but that's the way it is. If that won't work for you, a little fib won't hurt. You can say that we have company or that you have homework or that we're going out as a family. Whatever you'd like."

"It's not fair." Mira keeps arguing. "Kate gets to . . ."

"I make decisions based on what I think will be best for you," you reply calmly. "I understand that you want to be with your friends, and you may have dinner with them. That's it. If this isn't good enough for you, tell me now, and you'll eat dinner here. What's it going to be?"

"Pizza," Mira mumbles as she turns to walk away.

"Be home by six-thirty, please," you say. "And try to have a good time."

Mira isn't happy but you know she is aware of two things. One, you understand her desires and two, you place her safety above all else. She feels loved and thwarted. But that's okay. That's what being twelve is often about.

TECHNIQUE #21

A LITTLE PRIVACY, PLEASE

*WORKS FOR: DEALING WITH YOUR CHILD'S PLAY DATES—
DIARIES—SECRET PLACES—SPECIAL TOYS—
PHONE CONVERSATIONS—INNER THOUGHTS—
CURIOSITY ABOUT YOUR PRIVATE LIFE.*

THE TECHNIQUE

Think boundaries. Boundaries between you and your children and between each of your children, are a recognition that you are separate people. As a parent, this will mean many things:

- Containing your curiosity to "know" and your abundance of concern. If your child is whispering with a friend, don't ask what it's about. If she comes home very upset and doesn't want to talk, don't push.
- Making it clear many of her thoughts, feelings, and experiences do not *have* to be shared and if she desires to do so, that she can choose when and with whom she wishes to speak. "I can see you have things on your mind," you might say. "If you want to share them with me, I'd be happy to listen. I'm not going to push, though. You have a right to keep some things to yourself."

- Actively encouraging your child to safeguard her own personal space by letting her know certain belongings are entirely hers. Some things don't have to be shared with siblings. Certain toys or articles of clothing are completely under her control. Sharing with a sibling is nice. But don't overrate it. Allowing your children to "own" things is a way of teaching them to take responsibility for themselves as well.

- Being open to the moment when he says, "This is what happened." He has the right to choose the time that he's ready to reveal something about himself without meeting with your resentment or annoyance that he waited too long.

- Underlining your respect for your children as separate people by knocking on their doors before entering, not listening to phone conversations (unless it's clear there's something they want you to overhear), leaving locked diaries alone, and not sporadically rifling through their drawers.

- Allowing them to shut you out. Except they actually may not need you. If a child says, "I don't want to tell you what's bothering me. Let me call my friend," back off. Do not insist as if there should be nothing he can't tell you. Nothing you can't help with. There may very well be a situation you're better off staying away from! As a parent, you are hardly impartial!

- Recognizing those moments when your involvement is necessary and appropriate. Finding a pack of cigarettes in your twelve-year-old's drawer as you're putting away the laundry is not a time for respecting privacy. Privacy is a right, but it's also a privilege. A child cannot be allowed to abuse it, for his sake as well as yours.

By giving your child the sense that he can stand apart, you will also be doing yourself a favor. He will be more likely to instinctively understand your needs for privacy. Boundaries, in your family, will be a way of life.

WHY IT WORKS

It works because it gives your child what he needs.

As your child grows he needs to separate from you. It's a natural and healthy process but one with which he and you will experience much ambivalence. Still, this separation has to happen. If it doesn't, your child will grow up experiencing tremendous guilt, fear, and anger. Guilt and fear because he wants to pull away from you but feels he can't. That there's too much connection to you. That one or the both of you will fall apart if you separate. And anger, because everyone needs to be alone with himself. If he doesn't get the chance, he will feel invaded.

Setting up and modeling boundaries that protect the privacy of everyone in the family will help your child grow away from you in a way that will give him confidence, a strong sense of self, and a healthy respect for the boundaries of others.

When he gets to say a few toys belong only to him, you are empowering him. When you leave a diary alone, you are telling your child that even though you are his parent your rights over him are not unbounded. Knowing this will make it easier for him to share himself with you. And when you leave your child alone with his thoughts you are telling him that he is his person and that if he chooses to tell you what's on his mind you will listen because you want to help, not because you *ought* to know. You will be offering yourself as support, not as someone to whom he is beholden.

Respecting your child's privacy is an act of respecting him as an individual.

THE DEEPER MESSAGE

By allowing privacy, in the deepest sense you are expressing trust and your willingness to let him fly. You are telling your child that he can be his own person. He doesn't have to live like or for you, fill your every moment with his, or keep you happy with his neediness.

Giving your child privacy will leave him that much more able to turn to you freely when he feels the urge. He will not be in fear of being consumed by your needs or expectations. Nor will he feel chased or cornered. He will feel safe in the knowledge that to turn to you is not an act of giving something up, but rather an opportunity to learn, receive comfort, and feel loved.

You do not want a child who feels he has to parent you. It is a role he simply cannot fulfill, though try he might. Parenting can at times require a lot of involvement in a child's life. But sometimes it demands stepping back. Sometimes the best parenting is doing nothing at all.

SEEING IT IN ACTION:

Your Four-Year-Old

Just a few days ago, William received an extremely exotic Batmobile. It's silver and sleek and wondrously exciting.

The problem is that his six-year-old brother Sam is as enthralled by it as William, and for the most part you've had a rule in the house. Since so many of the same toys are attractive to each of them, everything must be shared.

You've noticed lately that this rule doesn't always work—that sometimes each of your children become infuriated, but it has seemed better than buying two of everything.

This Batmobile has once again brought the issue to the fore and something about each child's intransigence has made you aware the share rule may need to be refined.

William is shrieking, "It's mine! It's mine!" with such heartfelt anguish, that you have come to realize something very important.

He's right.

"Let's have a meeting," you say firmly, motioning for the children to sit down next to you on the floor.

"Here's the problem," you begin. "I've always said you should share things because you both like the same toys and I can't buy two of everything. Right?"

Both boys will probably nod and begin to protest.

"Wait," you go on. "But you were younger then and now you both are getting older and we all have to realize something. All of us in this house should really be entitled to some private property. Do you know what that means?''

Whether they say yes or no, explain. ''It means you should each have a few things that are completely under your control. Things you can lend or not, depending on how you feel.''

''Right,'' William•says quickly.

''But that means taking care of those things,'' you add. ''Keeping them private. William, if you leave the Batmobile in the playroom Sam is going to play with it. If you want it kept private, you must take care of it in your private space. Your room.''

''But that's not fair!'' Sam hollers.

''Well, Sam,'' you say quickly, ''Why don't you select a couple of things that you want to keep privately for yourself and that William can only play with if he asks permission. Okay?''

Then spend the next few minutes helping them each sort out a small list of toys they will claim as their own.

The sense of propriety they will feel may at first seem like selfish glee. But, in fact, you will be encouraging a sense of responsibility and pride. ''I,'' they will think, ''am the boss of something.'' It's a great feeling. It's a grown-up feeling.

It's a growth experience.

Your Eight-Year-Old

Nathan has been in the den by himself for about an hour. You have a sense that something went wrong on his play date with two friends, but he clearly doesn't want to talk. He was silent in the car and immediately after entering the house he went into the den and flipped on the television.

It hurts you terribly to see him so troubled. He's a sensitive child, though he doesn't always act that way, and when he's in pain, you can hardly stand it.

Unable to control yourself you walk into the den, and lower the volume on the television.

"Honey, I get the feeling something went wrong with Jacob and David today."

"I don't want to talk about it," Nathan replies, clearly upset and angry. "I want to watch TV."

"Watching television isn't going to solve anything," you plow forward. "Maybe if you talked to me you'd feel better."

"I don't want to talk," Nathan says, even louder now. "I just didn't have a good time. Okay?"

You will yourself to calm down . . . to see that your son is still in one piece. He's just upset. He's watching TV in all probability to comfort and distract himself. He's clearly not ready or willing to talk. Whatever happened is something for the time being he wants to own.

You are simply going to have to own your pain as well.

It's not his job to make you feel better about how he feels.

"Okay," you say quietly. "But I'd be happy to talk about things if you want to. Whenever." And then on the way out of the den, you lay your head gently on top of his head to express your love.

He may spill the beans later that night, by suddenly saying, "David and Jacob are mean," as an invitation to talk it through. Or he may not. He may wait until the morning or he may never tell you the details.

It may have been better for him to talk it through with you or it may not. But you shouldn't push your child to reveal himself if he chooses not to. You can only let him know you're available. If he is a child who keeps, you think, too much hurt to himself, you can try and model your willingness to talk out a problem whenever an appropriate situation presents itself (see technique #20). Relating an argument you had with a friend along with the resolution, could help him see how it's done without him having to reveal a thing.

Your Twelve-Year-Old

You are in your daughter Jennifer's room straightening up when you chance upon her open diary lying on the desk. Glancing down you see a passage that notes her friends have started smoking, and she's worried if she doesn't do it, too, she'll be considered uncool.

It's unclear to you if Jennifer might have wanted you to see this. Generally speaking, a closed diary in a child's room or really anywhere, means don't look. An open diary can sometimes mean a child needs help. But it's a touchy issue because there may be a great deal of ambivalence (the open diary is a sort of "accident") and you do not want to be accused of invading her privacy.

You decide just a little manipulation is in order (see technique #10). You bide your time for a day, and then find your opportunity one evening as you're flipping through a magazine in her presence.

"Someone should outlaw these sexy-looking cigarette ads," you say shaking your head. "I mean, don't they get it? Cigarettes kill people! Ask anyone!"

Your daughter shrugs.

"I was tempted when I was younger to try it because my friends did," you say casually. Actually, this is true. "But I decided not to because my parents had horrible coughs from it and people were starting to say it was really bad for you." You laugh. "I was embarrassed to not smoke, though, so I told my friends a relative had died of lung cancer and so I didn't want to do it. That kept them quiet."

Then smile and drop it. You will have given your daughter a tool to say "no" (it's easier to express a realistic fear than to moralize or offer an abstract "no" to peers) but successfully circumvented the diary issue at the same time.

Had the problem been a more serious one, such as reading that she is heavily experimenting with drugs, you would have had to put aside the privacy issue and simply, bluntly, put the facts to her. "I was in your room straightening up, your diary was open, I read the passage, and we have to talk."

Your child is entitled to privacy unless she is doing something dangerous to herself or others, or is engaged in illegal activities. As stated earlier, privacy is a right, but it is also a privilege extended to those who can handle it.

If your child is abusing his privacy, you have to step in.

TECHNIQUE #22

If There's a Loss, Let Him Be Sad

WORKS FOR: HELPING YOUR CHILD LEARN TO ACCEPT AND COPE CONSTRUCTIVELY WITH SAD TIMES SO THAT HE NEITHER DENIES HIS FEELINGS, NOR BECOMES OVERWHELMED BY THEM.

THE TECHNIQUE

When something sad happens, be it the death of a pet or a friend who is moving away, allow your child to feel it. Don't rush him away from the sadness. Don't immediately try and cheer him up.

Rather, acknowledge his feeling.

"It hurts to lose someone you love."

Discuss the feeling.

"I know you are remembering all kinds of things about Fluffy."

Just be there.

Allow your child, for a time, to simply cry while you sit by her.

Finally, after the sadness has been given its due, gently point out that it's always a good idea to try and make oneself feel better. And then discuss what some possibilities might be.

Be clear that you are not trying to forget about being sad, but rather trying to manage it.

"I know you're going to miss Fluffy a lot, and nothing we do will change that right now, but I do think you deserve to do something nice for yourself. Let's bake your favorite banana cake. It will help you feel a little better."

Finally, take into account your child's age. A very young child will tend not to stick with a sad moment very long, largely because he cannot anticipate the full impact of a loss. He will experience his sadness at different times and in different ways. It's important to allow a young child to set his own pace.

Central to this technique is your acceptance of sadness and your communicated expectation that your child should feel it.

WHY IT WORKS

Not only does this technique allow and encourage your child to consciously experience a sadness, but it lays the foundation for a healthy management of difficult feelings in the future.

By "teaching" your child to stick with the sadness you are helping him to face his feelings rather than bury them. You are protecting him from their inevitable re-emergence in the form of hostility or anxiety.

While it may be painful to watch your child hurting, you are embracing a situation that has finite parameters. When you speed him away too quickly from the unhappiness, you are protecting yourself from your child's pain. Not him. He will have the pain anyway, somehow, somewhere. In the end, ironically, you will have created a far more serious long-term problem: A child who cannot face his feelings.

Finally, when you help your child engage in some comforting activity you are very simply teaching him a coping mechanism. And that is, sadness can be balanced by a little pleasure. In fact, it ought to be.

THE DEEPER MESSAGE

Certainly you will want your child to have an upbeat feeling about life. But you will be doing your child a disservice not to recognize at appropriate and undeniable times that life is not always a joy. That it brings pain as well.

By encouraging your child to talk about his pain, you are gently teaching him that sorrow is a part of life. You cannot take it away from him. Nor do you want to. Certainly you don't like to see him hurting, but if the situation merits it, he has to "own" the feeling. There's no point pretending something isn't so.

Finally, by suggesting that your child find a way to comfort himself (with your help) you are telling your child that he should not allow himself to be overwhelmed or crippled by the feeling. He deserves to try and give himself some relief. This is not to ignore the sorrow, but rather to find a way to manage it better.

Sadness, you want your child to realize, is his right. But he does have a choice to make. Once he's acknowledged it he can wallow in it, or make room for other experiences that can inspire happier feelings.

Fluffy, the message should be, will never be forgotten. But life has to go on.

SEEING IT IN ACTION:

Your Four-Year-Old

Your daughter Megan has had two gerbils for the last couple of months. But suddenly, this morning, she woke up to find one of them dead.

You know she loved her gerbil Millie, but her reaction seems a bit odd to you. Megan looks surprised and unhappy, but also curious. A little lost even. There are, you notice, no tears.

"Megan, I think we should bury her and say a really nice good-bye to her. What do you think?" you say softly.

"Where?" Megan says. "In the ground?" She looks a little upset at that. Looking out the window she studies the snow on the front yard. "Won't she be cold?"

You're beginning to understand. Megan doesn't quite get it. The finality hasn't hit her, though something clearly has. Megan continues to look a bit shaken.

"Honey, Millie can't feel anything now. She died."

Megan looks at the tank. "Oh," she says softly.

You put your arm around her. "It's sad. I know you loved Millie."

"I want another gerbil!" Megan suddenly cries out.

This reaction, you know, is a combination of fear of loss and a desire to have things go back the way they were. Megan is trying to comfort herself and skip the empty feeling.

You meet her halfway.

"We'll get you another gerbil soon, Megan, but I

think right now we should bury Millie and say some nice things about her. Okay?''

''Yes,'' Megan says somberly. She dresses in her boots and coat while you go collect a shovel. The two of you go outside and you begin to dig a hole.

''Want to help?'' you ask her.

She does and then the two of you place Millie in the hole and cover her up.

''Millie,'' you begin, in an effort to help your child express herself, ''We will miss you. You were a friendly and loving gerbil.''

You look at Megan and smile. ''It's your turn.''

Megan looks down at the mound of dirt. ''You were very nice. You sat on my shoulder sometimes.'' She hesitates. ''You peed on me!'' and she laughs.

You laugh, too. Megan is achieving a balance she can handle.

You watch as she grows silent. ''My gerbil is in there,'' she says, suddenly, pointing to the spot.

You hug her. ''We'll always remember Millie.''

Megan nods. ''Can I have some hot chocolate?''

Your Nine-Year-Old

A very good friend of yours has just died. It was someone Peter knew very well. She had been sick a very short time, and so you are surprised and saddened.

You had warned Peter that she was very ill, and he had seemed, as you expected, very troubled by the news.

But now you have just had to tell him that she is gone.

Peter immediately stands up from his bed, where you have been sitting with him, and starts pacing around his room. He can't seem to find the toy he's looking for and so he goes downstairs. You hear him rummaging around in the playroom.

It's clear to you that he is looking for something to comfort himself, and that it is likely he will find nothing.

A few minutes later he comes back upstairs, empty-handed, sits down on the floor and starts fiddling with Legos.

"What do you remember the best about Alice?" you ask him gently.

"The books she brought me," he says immediately. "Also she was funny." He looks up at you. "How come she died?"

"She got sick. People get sick. And sometimes doctors can't fix them," you answer, knowing that's a scary piece of news.

"Are you going to her funeral?" Peter asks, still fiddling with the Legos.

"Yes. Do you want to come?" you ask.

"No," Peter replies quickly. Once again he stands up and starts searching through his shelves for a nonspecific item.

"I think you feel sad about Alice," you say.

Peter doesn't answer. He can't, you sense, get near it. It's too frightening.

You decide it's time to help him be less afraid of the feeling.

"You know, Peter, there are sad things in life and silly things, too. It's weird how they can exist at the same time, but they do. Should we remind ourselves of something silly, too?"

"Like what?" Peter asks, clearly mystified.

You take his hand and lead him into the bedroom where you turn on the cartoon channel. The two of you sit and watch for five minutes during which time you both laugh. Then you turn off the TV.

"That was silly, right?"

Peter nods.

"And Alice dying is sad. Right?"

He nods again.

"That's what I mean," you say, putting your arm around him.

"I wish she were still alive," Peter says, leaning against you.

"I do, too," you say, stroking his cheek. "We will miss her a lot."

A few tears escape from your eyes and you wipe them away, but not because you are concerned that Peter will see them. You are having an appropriate reaction. And he is, too.

Your Twelve-Year-Old

Angela's best friend has just moved and your daughter is now going to start sixth grade with a giant hole in her life. She's been moping around the house for about a week now, and your sense is that things are getting out of hand.

You talked to her about Janie leaving and how it must feel. You held Angela's hand as she cried, and you tried cheering her up a bit by buying her a few extra things with which to begin school, including a terrific pair of jeans, and taking her to the movies twice.

But Angela seems bent on feeling miserable, not to mention sorry for herself. The time has come, you think, for her to pull herself together and find a way to make the best of what's happened. She needn't forget Janie, of course, but she does have to open herself up to the possibility of new good times.

You find her in her bedroom Saturday morning, reading a magazine. She should, you firmly feel, be out with her other friends.

"Angela," you say, walking in and sitting on her bed. Your tone is now matter-of-fact. Not as nurturing or gentle as it has been. "You ought to get together with your friends."

"I don't want to. It's not the same," she replies.

"So, because things are not the same, they can't still be good?" you ask. "How sad for you."

"What's that supposed to mean?" Angela asks sharply.

"I mean it's sad for you. Janie leaving is upsetting, absolutely. But you can still keep up a relationship with her. And in the meantime you have a life to live here. And Janie has one to live where she is. You can miss each other. But sitting home all the time is just going to make it worse."

"I don't know . . ." Angela sighs heavily. "I miss her."

"Well, I do know. I think you need to do two things. One, do something to make sure you and Janie stay friends, and two, go out and have a good time with other people." Walking over to her desk you bring back some paper and a pen. "Write her a letter. Tell her what's on your mind. Then get off the bed and call someone."

"I don't . . ."

"I know it's hard," you say, a little more gently now. "But you have a choice. You can give in to feeling nothing but sadness, and have no fun at all, or you can be sad and move forward anyway so that you can still have some fun. It's your life. You are not the first person to have to cope with someone dear moving away.''

And with that you walk out of her room.

Angela doesn't stir for about a half hour. But then you hear her pick up the phone in the hallway.

About ten minutes later she appears in her jacket.

''I'm meeting Sally,'' she says with a little smile.

''Good.'' You smile back noticing the stamped envelope in her hand.

''Have a good time,'' you add.

''Maybe,'' she says and then walks away. Angela is definitely feeling a little sorry for herself. But also scared at having lost someone so important to her. She is going to have to reorganize her friendships and probably the thought is daunting.

But that's okay. Life brings losses and changes. Angela is starting to learn that. And even the people who love her the most, such as you, will not want to pat her shoulder forever. She is expected to get on with it.

Like everyone else does.

TECHNIQUE #23

THE RIGHT TO PROTECT YOURSELF

*WORKS FOR: AN ANGRY OR MOODY CHILD WHO IS
SNAPPING AT YOU, BEING GRUMPY AND UNCOOPERATIVE,
SPREADING A CLOUD AROUND THE HOUSE*

THE TECHNIQUE

Most children (and many adults) have trouble directly handling their hurt or anger. These are unpleasant feelings and are often left unexplored. Instead, children "act out," or express their unhappiness by striking out where they feel safest.

At home, and at you.

This can be debilitating to a family. You will want to express your awareness that your child is upset about something, but that it is not permissible to take it out on everyone around him. How you get your point across will depend on your child's age but essentially this is what you need to communicate.

"I can see something is bugging you. I'm happy to talk about it with you. But I won't allow you to yell at me for no reason, or mistreat anyone in the family. If you can't control yourself, and you don't want to talk, please go to your room until you can behave reasonably.

Try listening to some music or maybe even writing down what you're so angry about . . .''

Do try and stay away from consequences, however. When your child's poor behavior is a direct result of a painful problem, he deserves a little slack. Learning to deal directly with pain as opposed to striking out is a difficult lesson and one that deserves your patience and understanding.

And do remember not to take his behavior personally. Some parents feel hurt and resentful when a child attempts to roll over them like a bulldozer. But your child's inappropriate expression of his pain is about him, not you. And, in fact, it's an expression of his trust. You simply have to stand firm and let him know you are a person, too. Not a whipping post.

WHY IT WORKS

Your child is likely feeling out of control. He's clearly distressed about something, and rather than face it head-on, he is striking out everywhere.

This can't feel good. By setting up boundaries, you are helping him take hold of himself, and get closer to what it is exactly that is disturbing him. When you say, ''I understand something is bothering you,'' you are reminding him that, in fact, something in particular is! Something he might rather forget but which he has to think about.

Or, at the very least, you are containing and protecting him from himself. When you refuse to let him ''loose'' you are underlining your ability to take care of him.

Whether you decide to leave the den where he is

growling endlessly, or you send him to his room because he won't stop slamming kitchen cabinets and snapping at everything you say, you are telling him that striking out isn't going to help. He's simply going to have to find another way.

And he will. Whether it's a quietly sought-out conversation with you, or a call to a friend, hitting a pillow, or reading a good book, the boundaries will help him focus on the task at hand.

Finding a constructive way to feel better.

THE DEEPER MESSAGE

This is an opportunity to help your child begin drawing on his inner resources.

As much as we might want to protect our children from the realities of life, they will have to see that there are many things they can't control. Things happen. They can only control their own reactions. They can fume, or they can choose to do something to help themselves feel better.

By refusing to allow your child to ignore the real problem, which is his pain and what to do about it, you are helping him look inward. By telling him that you are willing to talk, you are letting him know that's one way to get through his difficult feelings. That he is not alone. And by suggesting ways for him to make himself feel better, you are essentially telling him "I know that you have the strength to get through whatever it is that's bothering you. I think you can comfort yourself."

And finally you are telling your child that no matter what his feelings, you will not tolerate the mistreatment.

You are a person, you have feelings, too, and you need to have your boundaries respected.

It is one thing for family members to expect to receive consistent support and love from each other. It is quite another for them to assume, therefore, that ''anything goes.''

It doesn't. And if your child learns that at home, he is more likely to treat everyone outside of the family circle with the respect they deserve as well.

SEEING IT IN ACTION:

Your Four-Year-Old

Stephanie is extremely upset. You have just picked her up from a very unsuccessful play date. Her friend Meredith, a rather aggressive little girl, had bossed Stephanie around for most of the afternoon. The baby-sitter apologized when you picked Stephanie up and while you are slightly annoyed at her for not calling you sooner, you're more preoccupied by Stephanie's demeanor.

There are tears in her eyes, but she looks intensely angry. On the car ride home you try to talk to her about what happened but all she will say is ''I hate Meredith.'' You gently respond, ''You must be very angry,'' but Stephanie continues to sit sullenly and quietly in the car without responding.

Finally you get her home where she proceeds to rampage around the playroom, supposedly looking for her Barbie. In fact, she is clearly enjoying the feeling of tossing her toys around the room, creating a big mess.

"Boy, I certainly hope you intend to clean this up," you say gently.

"NO," Stephanie cries out. "I'm not going to do that."

"Honey, I think you are very upset about your play date with Meredith," you offer sympathetically.

"NO I'M NOT!" Stephanie insists.

She's very young. Too young to intellectually understand the principle of sublimation. But not too young to sense that you know what she's feeling. "I think you are. And I think that's why you're throwing things all around," you say gently. "It makes you feel better to throw something."

"NO, I JUST WANT MY BARBIE!"

Your eyes survey the room quickly and finally alight on the doll. Knowing this is not what Stephanie really wants, you extend it to her anyway, realizing it will go some ways toward keeping her from throwing anything else in the air. This is one way for you to set a boundary.

"Here you go, honey," you say softly. "You can stop throwing things around now. I think Meredith wasn't nice to you today, and it made you very upset. But you know it's better to say, 'I'm REALLY mad' than to break your toys. Breaking stuff doesn't help when you're upset."

Stephanie looks away.

"Come help me clean up the room," you say as you begin to scoop up the toys.

Stephanie halfheartedly picks up a few toys.

"Sometimes when I get really mad I scrunch up my face like this and hit a pillow," you go on.

Grimacing, you hand her a throw pillow from the sofa.

Stephanie looks at it tentatively and gives it a swat. Then she smiles, and hits it again. Harder this time.

Your Nine-Year-Old

You have just brought your nine-year-old home from his second baseball game of the season. He's not particularly athletic, but he's a competent hitter and most of the time enjoys himself.

Unfortunately it was a bad day. He could neither hit nor catch well and as a result is feeling extremely embarrassed. He refused to speak at all on the ride home, sullenly looking out the window while two of his teammates whom you were dropping off, chattered endlessly about the game.

Your son is now looking in the refrigerator, it's almost dinnertime and he is pulling out a cupcake.

"Uh-uh," you say matter-of-factly. "We're about to eat dinner. You can have that for dessert. But not right now."

"I want it now . . ." he hisses between gritted teeth.

"I understand that. I also understand you had a bad game today and you feel terrible about it. But, honey, you've had a bunch of good practices, your first game was good and this . . ."

"I don't care about the game," Peter practically shrieks. "Leave me alone." He puts the cupcake back. And slams the refrigerator shut.

Just then his younger brother Sam walks in and gleefully calls out, "Hi, Peter! You know what?! I made this big castle in the play . . ."

"WHO CARES!" Peter yells at him. "Castles are stupid!"

Sam's lower lip begins to quiver. "They are not, they . . ."

"Castles are wonderful," you assure him. "Very special and solid and you made a beautiful one."

"It probably is as stupid as . . ." Peter interrupts.

"Enough," you say firmly. You rest both hands on Peter's shoulders. "Listen to me. I realize you're disappointed about the game. It's put you in a very bad mood. When things don't go the way we want them to we all get upset. But it doesn't mean you have a right to pick fights with me or your brother. Now, if you want to talk about the game fine, or if you want to just calm down and be pleasant that's okay, too. But if you're going to stomp around the kitchen like an ogre, then please go up to your room until you can pull yourself together."

"I don't want to go to my room . . ." Peter snaps. "I hate you."

"No you don't," you insist calmly. "You hate the way the game went. I'm not sending you to your room to punish you. I'm sending you so that you can't attack Sam and me and so that maybe you can gather your thoughts so we can talk, or so you can do something you enjoy. Like play with your computer."

Peter appears to be a little less agitated now. On top of a bad game he hadn't wanted to feel shunned as well.

"Maybe I'll go upstairs and take off my uniform," he says unhappily.

"Fine," you agree. "I'll call you when dinner is ready if you're not down by then." You tousle his hair a bit. "Mickey Mantle had bad days, too, you know," you say softly.

Your Twelve-Year-Old

Ever since Maria walked in the house from school she's been looking for a fight. You have no idea what happened, not for want of asking, of course, but something definitely did.

Maria keeps insisting, "Nothing's wrong! Leave me alone." But, of course, you can't leave her alone because she's clearly embarked on a trip down, "Let's Get On Mom's Nerves Lane," complete with leaving her snack plate on the table instead of putting it in the sink, announcing she lost her homework assignment, throwing her shoes on the steps, and glaring at you every moment while she pretends to leaf through a magazine.

You're about to really let loose when it occurs to you this is just what she wants. An opportunity to get into a knockdown battle so that she can use up all of her angry energy.

The trouble is once she does this you will not have helped her learn to work out a problem. Instead, she'll have had a grand exercise in venting.

So instead of indignantly putting her in her place, you call it as you see it.

"You know, Maria, it's clear something happened at school today. I don't know what it was and I'd certainly be happy to talk about it but you don't seem to want to do that. It seems you'd rather pick a fight with me. So I'll tell you what I'm going to do. I have work to finish in my office. If I can't help, call a friend, or write in your diary or do whatever you can to help yourself feel better. You can't control what other people do, but you can certainly control how you handle what they do. For example,'' you can add with a smile, "I can't control the mood you're in. But I can certainly remove myself from your presence so that we don't get into a silly fight. Speaking of which, please pick up your shoes and put your plate in the sink.''

And with that you walk out of the kitchen into the safety of your office. You feel pretty good, too. You weren't able to help your daughter by talking with her, but you were able not to add to her troubles by fighting with her. And, importantly, you made it clear that finding a way to comfort oneself is a very good thing.

TECHNIQUE #24

DON'T FORGET TO APOLOGIZE

WORKS FOR: SHOWING YOUR CHILDREN THAT YOU RESPECT THEM—CONFIRMING THEIR ABILITY TO ASSESS REALITY— LETTING THEM SEE YOU DON'T FEEL YOU'RE PERFECT.

THE TECHNIQUE

Don't avoid the words, "I'm sorry I..."

If you were short-tempered or made a snap, misguided judgment, say so. If you hurt your child's feelings unintentionally, an "I'm sorry. I was insensitive," or "I wasn't thinking," is good. Your child has likely heard you accuse him of the same. It will be enlightening to see you feel yourself capable of the same mistakes.

If you overreact to a child's behavior and respond in an unnecessarily hurtful or angry way, admit it free and clear before you point out your child's part in the problem. Don't say, "I'm sorry I slammed the door in your face but you've got to stop asking me when you can have a new pair of skis." Do say, "It was wrong of me to slam the door in your face. It's a very unkind and rude thing to do. The trouble is I get very upset when you keep at me about something when I don't have a clear answer. Skis cost a lot of money and I'm not sure I can spare it now."

And finally, remember, it is as important to apologize to a four-year-old as it is a twelve-year-old. It is never too early to begin the work of helping your child assess reality, and learn he deserves respect.

WHY IT WORKS

An apology builds bridges. It's a way of restoring good feelings between you and your child. And it's an excellent model. If your child senses that you can apologize with forthrightness and ease, then he will likely find it easier himself to do the same.

Many people feel too ashamed to apologize. They prefer to walk about either filled with guilt, or consumed with the fruitless task of convincing themselves of their innocence. By saying you are sorry, you are displaying the importance of being honest about one's own behavior—a certain acceptance that mistakes are something everybody makes—and the ease that one can feel at owning up to having made one.

THE DEEPER MESSAGE

You are admitting to your child that you are not all-knowing. You are fallible. It also confirms his sense of self-worth and perspective on a situation. Chances are he thinks you were out of line. When you apologize, you help him trust his ability to analyze a situation. You teach him to have faith in his own judgments.

And in terms of your relationship, an apology affords your child the chance to clearly see you respect his rights. Children often feel as if they are second-class citizens and there's nothing to be done about it except periodically rebel.

Your apology is a clear message that you do respect his right to be treated fairly and well.

SEEING IT IN ACTION:

Your Four-Year-Old

It's an extremely cold day and you are about to leave the house with your son Ben. It's taken way too long for him to get dressed but you forced yourself to be patient. Ben is trying very hard to achieve some independence.

You are waiting by the front door while he goes to fetch his down parka. Instead, he rounds the corner wearing what you know is his favorite coat—a bright blue midweather number appropriate for fifty-degree weather.

You've had it. "Ben," you snap. "Go back and get your winter jacket. NOW."

"But it's not there," Ben whimpers. "I looked."

"Of course it's there," you insist angrily. "If you want to get dressed yourself, fine. But then you have to think about how cold it is. Now go get your parka!"

"IT ISN'T THERE!" Ben yells. "I TOLD YOU!"

"Don't be ridiculous. We always hang it up," you argue, stamping down the hall to the hooks where the children's coats hang. "If I find that coat I'm going to be so . . ."

It isn't there. And in a flash you remember why. It's

in your car, where Ben had slipped it off the day before because he was too hot.

You turn to see Ben glaring at you full of an appropriate "I told you so," self-righteousness.

His eyes, however, look a bit teary.

"Ben," you say, bending down toward him. "Daddy was wrong. I should have believed you. The parka is in the car where you left it."

"I TOLD YOU," Ben proclaims. The tears are now making their way down his cheeks.

"Yes you did." You confirm his reality. "You did, and I said that wasn't true. But it was true. You're right to be angry that I wouldn't listen."

Ben nods energetically.

"Come," you say, taking his hand. "Let's go to the garage. We'll put your coat on in the car. Okay? And next time I'll listen to what you're saying. You're a smart boy and you know what you're talking about."

Ben takes your hand. "That's right," he says.

Your Ten-Year-Old

Your ten-year-old daughter Janie has just walked in from baseball practice after a long day at school. She is clearly exhausted.

But so are you. You had a difficult day at the office, and you had come home a little early in the hopes of getting her started on the history project that is due next week.

"Hi, Janie," you say the moment she's in the door. "Wash up, eat some dinner, and let's get started on the assignment." You continue sorting through the mail.

"I'm so tired . . ." Janie sighs.

"I can see that," you say tersely. "But if you'd started this project earlier it might not be so necessary to plunge in tonight. So go clean up."

"I have other homework," Janie groans, hovering by your side. "Can't we start tomorrow? I can come home straight from school."

"NO WE CANNOT!!" You slam your hand down on the counter, clearly in a fury. "THIS HAPPENS ALL OF THE TIME. YOU GET NOTHING DONE ON TIME. I DON'T CARE HOW TIRED YOU ARE. MARCH. I'M NOT COMING HOME EARLY TO-MORROW NIGHT."

"I hate you!" Janie cries out as she turns and flies up to her room.

You look down at the mail, seething. But a few moments later the guilt begins to seep in.

You could have handled that differently. Sure, Janie is chronically late attacking her projects. But she was understandably exhausted and you had pounced the moment she walked in the door. Chances are, if you'd given her a little room, and let her refresh herself, she'd have found the energy to begin the work.

Instead you'd created, due to your own tension, a huge argument.

After taking a few deep breaths, you go upstairs and knock on Janie's door.

"Go away," she barks.

"I'd like to talk to you, honey," you say, trying hard to convey that the screaming, at least from your side, is over.

"What is it?" she says just a touch less belligerently.

You open the door.

"First of all, I want to apologize for jumping on you

this evening. I'd had a bad day and was very tense. You were clearly tired and I should have lightened up when I saw you."

Janie shrugs.

"The thing is, though, Janie, we've been through this before. You do tend to put your big projects off, and that's a problem. I think we should proceed as planned even if we don't get as much done as I'd hoped. What do you say? After you've had a good dinner, of course!"

Janie shrugs again. "Okay. We could do some . . ."

"Great," you respond calmly. "I was wrong to light into you like that. I'm glad we're going to try and move ahead."

Forgive Yourself

WORKS FOR: REMINDING YOURSELF THAT NO ONE IS A PERFECT PARENT.

THE TECHNIQUE

Recognize that no matter how many books you read, parenting magazines you scour, or lectures you attend, you will not parent perfectly. Nobody does. You have your own set of problems that are going to impact on the way in which you deal with your children. And your children are monumental testers. It is their want to push you to the edge.

You are bound to make less than ideal decisions, say unnecessary things, and generally botch a pivotal confrontation.

The important thing is to then go back and try to rectify whatever it is you have wrought. If you've imposed too strict a punishment, lessen it. If you've exaggerated your child's wrongdoing, let him see you are putting it back into perspective. And if you've misread what your child needs from you, go back and give him what he requires.

"I shouldn't have jumped so quickly to say you can't go on that camping trip. I was nervous. But I found out a number of parents are going. Not just two. You may go. I should have checked into everything a little more thoroughly. But you know? I'm not perfect. Nobody is.''

Children are more resilient than most parents give them credit for. If they get the love they need, and your blunders are neither extreme nor frequent, they can take the bumpy ride. Children don't need perfect parents to be well-adjusted. But they do need parents who stay on top of the job.

In other words, forgive yourself and then move forward. Don't wallow in guilt. Don't beat yourself up. Don't give up.

WHY IT WORKS

First, you want to feel like a good parent. If you don't forgive yourself for your mistakes, you will not be able to view yourself in a positive light.

Second, if you hang onto the guilt, your children will be able to manipulate. They will pick up on your remorse, and try and do what kids do best. Get away with as much as they can!

Third, by not making every mistake you make into a cause célèbre, you resist treating your children like hothouse flowers. They need to know unfair moments will be visited upon them. They need to know you assume they can survive. They need to be given some credit for knowing that you are basically on their side.

THE DEEPER MESSAGE

Your children will learn not to seek perfection in themselves when they see you can admit your mistake, fix it, and then let it go with an acknowledgment that you're not perfect.

You are telling your child it is acceptable to err, but not to then walk away. Efforts should be made to remedy the problem. No one should expect to do everything perfectly.

But that fact should not convey permission to shrug one's shoulders and say, "Ah well," as if to err is your due.

It is not. It is merely the part of being human that needs work.

This principle should hold true for every technique in this book. No parent can apply them to their best advantage every time. A particularly vexing day, an extremely irascible child, a confusing situation, or misunderstood exchange can all contribute to a most unproductive confrontation and unsatisfactory resolution.

But that's okay. When you've had a chance to take a deep breath you can always go back and try to straighten things out. In a household filled with basic goodwill and love, people of all ages can bounce back from just about everything.

These techniques are designed to not only make your lives together easier, but to protect the rights and integrity of everyone in the home.

It's not that you have to do everything just right.

It's that you have to go at it with the belief that both you and your child deserve each other's respect and attention always.